All That the Locusts Have Eaten:

God's Redemption through Loss and Heartache

Chuck Carr

Send inquiries and letters to the author at:
Chuck Carr
P.O. Box 241
Crabtree, Pa 15624
Owner may also be found at Chuck-Carr.com

The Library of Congress has catalogued this manuscript as follows:
Carr, Charles Robert, 2020

For more information, blog topics, and other books, visit Chuck-Carr.com

First Printing: July 2020

The incidents in this book are told from my perspective only. Any conversations have been recreated to the best of my recollection. Others may recall these events differently.

Contents

Preface

This book is dedicated to all of us who are at our wit's end, those of us who are searching for answers that we cannot find. It is written to the countless souls among us who scratch their heads daily, wondering how in the world we have gotten ourselves into such a mess. To those whose fairytale lives appear to be crashing into disaster; to the men and women, boys and girls, whose dreams seem to be shattered or broken into pieces. This book is written to those of us in an almost disastrous place.

If this describes your current condition, then you are one of many that my heart breaks for. My intentions in this book are to open the eyes of those who need help. Even in a state of chaos, there is hope for you. I desperately want to open your eyes to see that light is out there for you, shining right at the end of the proverbial tunnel. I wrote this to allow you to glean from a different perspective, to bring lasting value and help to you in this incredibly hard time. As a book illuminating bright light, this book is meant to help the hurting, giving you the chance to see a glimmering flicker of hope in the midst of your crisis. Yes, hope. If I can convince anyone who reads this book to see the hope that still awaits you, to convince any feeble legs to continue to stand, or to give an ounce of strength to the starving soul who has no strength left to keep going on, then all my efforts will have been worthwhile.

This book is dedicated to you. I know exactly how you feel—not because I know who you are, but because I have been there myself. I have worn your shoes with my own feet. This book is written to give you courage, strength, and hope. Somehow, someway, I want God to use what has happened to me to restore hope and strength in someone else's life as well. I would be overjoyed if that someone were you.

Without hope, we lose sight of value. In my estimation, nothing is more fundamentally vital to the human spirit than hope. It is the essence of what drives us to carry on. Without it, we are lost and searching without direction, but with it, we can find strength and see through to the end. Hope is the flicker of light in the darkest of times. It is the slight whispering scent of tasteful nourishment to the hungry and starving soul. Hope keeps us pushing forward. With it, the Lord brings us to greater places.

I do feel a certain freedom inside to express myself candidly. Although my hardships in life might seem slight to those in the global persecuted church, those who have seen wartime conflict and battle, or those who fight debilitating disease or pain, writing this book has certainly not come easily to me. I paid an enormous personal price to pen these words, a very real struggle with a high cost. Yet I feel as Paul did when he wrote that I can certainly boast in my weakness. Second Corinthians 12:9–10 is a priceless passage to me: "But he said to me, 'My grace is sufficient for you, for my power is made perfect in weakness.' Therefore I will boast all the more gladly of my weaknesses, so that the power of Christ may rest upon me. For the sake of Christ, then, I am content with weaknesses, insults, hardships, persecutions, and calamities. For when I am weak, then I am strong."

With this passage in mind, I am not afraid or ashamed to tell my story, my testimony, the way God walked me through everything. As Paul, I have reason to boast, not due to anything good or great about myself but because Christ has been visibly glorified in me. Since the Lord has healed my heart, mind, and soul of the hurts and scars written about in this book, I no longer have any reason to keep these matters to myself. For with my testimony, Christ will shine for others to see. The stories and lessons in these pages will help thousands of people who are hurting from similar situations. For that, I am forever grateful.

In writing *All That the Locusts Have Eaten*, some segments and stories in my testimony include other people. I have made great attempts to speak of every situation without condescension or disparagement. I believe that Christian literature has no room for that. I also believe that God can restore any situation, and so I do not want to make myself any higher or lower than anyone else. We are all human, and we all make mistakes. Sometimes those mistakes affect others. Even the best of intentions can backfire, so we need to give some room and grace for personal redemption and to allow God to restore a situation.

I have omitted the names of people involved in the stories I tell to protect the future promise of God's grace and dignity to each and every one of us. In saying that, I do, however, truly believe these stories can be used for good, so I have included them. Too many hurting people out there beyond my immediate circle of influence need to read all of what I've lived through. All I aim to do is speak my testimony, which is exactly what this book is designed to do.

Many situations and stories out there are far worse than what I endured. If this is you, I do not downplay your experience at all. I merely write from my own perspective and trust that my life can bring hope to someone else. This book is simply what I have learned from my *own* journey, what *I* have come away with, and what the Lord has taught *me* in my wilderness wanderings. It is simply my testimony, a collection of writings that explain what I have learned *personally*.

Many routes may lead to the end of what the Lord has taught and revealed to me. This is simply the way God walked *me* through it. In that, I hope to inspire you to grasp his mighty hand with the humble confidence that he will carry you though your situation as well. This book is not meant to glorify me, my level of spiritual maturity, or to make my story seem like a Shakespeare play. I only wrote it for the hope that lies within me and to give you hope as well.

If God can carry me through all the struggles of life, he most certainly can do the same for you. My prayer, as you read this book, is that somehow, I can point others to see the gracious hands that are open and ready to hold you even in the midst of your own personal struggle. The Good Shepherd's rod is willing and eager to guide you. The Father is ready to embrace and comfort you. The God of all creation, who has already asked to carry your burden, is more than capable of holding you during this time. If I can point just one soul to the Lord who longs for all this and more, then this book—and my challenging story as I lived it—was not written in vain.

So to you who search for light when there are no answers, I have searched also. To you who cry in the night when you have no strength to carry on, my tears join yours. To the soul who wants to grab God by the collar and give him a piece of your mind, I've already done that. Trust me. I get it. I know exactly where you are coming from. To you, this book is written, and to you, I propose this question: "Will you give God the opportunity to show you how good he really is?" My great desire is that I can help you do just that. One of my favorite Scriptures of all time sums it up perfectly. "Taste and see that the Lord is good" (Psalm 34:8 KJV).

Will you have a taste today? Are you willing to try a sample? Will you reach out and make even a small effort to taste the Lord's goodness? May the words that I've penned from my heart encourage you to do the same. May your hurting heart hear mine and look to the Lord of light.

Introduction

Some readers may say that the book of Joel was written as a prophetic word only, warning readers of the coming day of the Lord and encouraging them to prepare for it via the call of repentance. This is true. But what I want to glean from this book is that it illustrates a simple principle that can be found in so many other places throughout Scripture that I simply don't have time to recount them all. Joel just happens to be the most concise and simplest reference to me because the concepts are all illustrated in one short book. A common theme can be found in Genesis, Isaiah, Psalms, Judges, Job, and many other books. One Scripture in particular, which I will reference later, is Psalm 107, which I have grown to love. This sweet, soothing, and balmy passage can calm the weary soul that is not yet out of the deep water.

Through many references and passages in the Bible with recurring themes, we find the simple message that God can restore us when we find ourselves in deep affliction, elevating us to a place of safety and security when we cry out to him. He will not leave the destitute in

11

despair. He will not let the righteous cry without answering their prayers in some form or fashion. He is gentle and slow to anger.

Yes, he does correct us when needed, but those of us who find ourselves in a mess that we really did nothing to deserve, well, that is a different matter. When tragedy strikes simply due to living in a fallen world, we can cry out to our Father with the knowledge that he has helped countless others before us, and as patterned in Scripture, we can be restored from all that the locusts have eaten. Also, the wonderful news about our God is that even if we are at fault, thus bringing hardships and struggles on ourselves as we justly deserve, a heart that turns to the Lord can still receive a wonderful blessing of restoration and a beautiful ending.

With a sad heart, I must say that sometimes Christians can be the most difficult people to be around when you are really hurting. The book of Job clearly describes and illustrates that those who seem to be righteous around us may be the very ones who hurt the most. When answers cannot be found for the searching and suffering soul, we, as Christians, often place the guilt and burden on the sufferer, saying it must be their own fault. We foolishly conclude that they must have done something to bring suffering and hardships on themselves. We mistakably think that they harbor something inside their own hearts to cause all this. That type of mentality, in my opinion, is both inaccurate and cowardly. We can easily blame someone when we pray for them yet don't see the answered results of healing in their lives. It's an easy out and shifts the blame off us— who don't understand why we aren't being heard—to the one suffering, leaving us guilt-free. We don't have to put in the hours of prayer on our knees to get the job done.

We like being a microwave society. When our prayers don't seem to be answered, we can give up. We conclude that the person we are praying for isn't being rescued or healed and that it's their own fault. What a shameful approach to helping the hurting and needy. We, as Christians, should not stoop to the level of Job's three friends. They really should have just rolled up their sleeves and gotten into the trenches with him, but they instead looked down on him. We live in a fallen world. It's that simple. Don't make more of it than it is.

God has the unbelievable ability to take any hardship or bad event and turn it around for his glory and for the benefit of those who believe in him. He does it all the time. I hope that this book allows the readers to see and believe that. Countless times in history, even in biblical history, God takes horrible circumstances and turns them around, making beautiful artwork. The life of Joseph is just one example. (See Genesis 39–50.) A fallen world cannot muster up anything that God can't use for his glory. If you have been wounded in the past, take comfort, because there were plenty of examples in Scripture of wounded people as well, and they became victorious overcomers. This book will help you be one too.

I also want to take a moment to say point blank, that I do believe in divine healing. God can heal one person as easily and quickly as you can say the word "healed." I have read about and seen healings take place. My own grandmother was healed at a young age by God of cancer and went on to live a full, long, and wonderful life. Her story alone indirectly allows me to be here today to tell my own story. God heals. This is an indisputable fact.

The purpose of this book, however, is to explain that God's ways are not our ways, and our thoughts are not always God's thoughts. Sometimes, his idea of healing differs from ours. Sometimes, he may heal someone in ways that outside observers cannot comprehend or reason with. Does that make his ways any less perfect than if we would receive the results we desire, ask for, or expect? Absolutely not! Sometimes God just has a different plan in mind than we do.

I pray that this book will allow readers to see that God is God, and God is always good, and we should not blame him when life doesn't turn out as we would like it to. Rather, we should adjust our thinking to view the situation as God does. This does not and should not change our prayers for what we want or desire to see happen. It is simply a gracious and proper perspective and another consideration in times when he does not.

I am a living testimony to that prayer and response. My life clearly represents God taking unfortunate circumstances and turning them into something good. Romans 8:28 is my motto. I've lived it. I've breathed it. Although it took about fifteen years for my personal situation to begin to turn around, I've seen God do exactly what he stated and promised in that verse. He can do the same for you. My job is to point you to Jesus, showing you that God is never blindsided or surprised by anything that happens, and to encourage you to keep pressing into him instead of running away from him.

For this reason, I started Life Compass Ministries. I hope to show a hurting world that God is still in the business of healing, restoration, and renewal. He will restore all that the locusts have eaten to the hungry soul who turns to him for answers. More than that, he will himself become the answer. He truly is the "I AM."

To my family, past, present, and future.
The message I wish to pass on.

With Love,
Chuck

Chapter 1
Before the Flood
(The Plague Begins)

Dost thou love life? Then do not squander time,
for that is the stuff life is made of.
~ Benjamin Franklin

A valley stood before him. Beauty and color filled his eyes. He exhaled a sigh of satisfied relief, then breathed in deeply the inspiration that dazzled everything around. A morning bright and boldly filled of sweet sunshine, warming all who caught the blanket rays of warmth, glazed his skin with the freshest sense of life itself. He faced the pleasant valley, wide-eyed in its glory. The scent of lush spring grass hinted at life in full swing. It tickled the toes—sensitive, tender, and soft, energizing those members who dared to bare their skin in its freshness and chill.

Wildflowers bloomed in every direction, bringing the subconscious drift of relaxation and stillness in a world where only abundance flowed. A river ran through the land, flowing with a life of abundant crystal, chilled water to those thirsty nearby, and the soft trickling of a symphony orchestra of natural peace. Precious creations, boasting their own specialized vibrant colors of glory, popped against a lush green backdrop. Vibrant reds and yellows burst forth with vivid pigment and sparkle. God had used the entire palette to paint this sky, the valley, this landscape. Not a leaf fell to the ground. Instead, each clung with firm vigor to the sap blood of life. The great behemoth arms of branched trees graced and lined the riverbank, the meadow stream in cushioned shade.

Peace surrounded him. He closed his eyes. Even so, this dwelling place of comfort and warmth, full of the best goodness the Lord could wrap around him, could be seen and enjoyed without the use of open eyes. It was enough to be alive, for his whole life was good. Life was precious, and that—well-watered, nurtured, and lived.

§

Believe it or not, at one time, my life was not very dramatic. Those who know me well might not remember those days, but truthfully, the illustration of a green, peaceful meadow was really the life I lived. The days of lush green grass and rays of sunshine were very sweet to me. I did love life. I was not squandering time. I was drinking life in with all that I had and was doing quite well at it. I felt as though my life were a dream; the world was my oyster. It seemed as if things couldn't get any better. I was living the ideal life that I had always wanted growing up, a life graced with green and flowers. The

Lord had put me in such a pleasant place, and everywhere I looked, his hand was doing wonderful things. I was young but was growing and walking in his ways, and he was leading me in this sweet land of promise.

I suppose that I am a rare breed. I did not have the rough childhood of dysfunction that so many other children unfortunately face nowadays. I was quite blessed, in fact. Both my biological parents raised me with a strong sense of family and faith. I was the oldest of five children. In many ways, my experiences spearheaded the path for many others, especially my siblings. The five of us were raised on a family-owned and -operated dairy farm near the small town of Crabtree, Pennsylvania.

I was constantly surrounded and immersed in nature, as much of what was all around inspired me to use and develop the talents of drawing, painting, and writing. It was not only a beautiful place to live, but the farm also provided me with a sense of stability, the framework for a strong work ethic, and the avenue of good old-fashioned fun that kept me out of trouble. Most days, I was too busy to get into mischief, and I spent my free time with siblings and cousins who lived on nearby farms. Our days were filled with adventure and excitement. Farm kids know how to find fun, and we lived it to the full.

§

As a teenager, I tried to stay on course as best I could. Some teenagers feel as if they have to rush into romantic relationships with the opposite sex at this age. I never felt that way. I was content with the life the Lord gave me each day and took whatever it brought me in stride. I was not very interested in dating women who weren't potential marriage partners. I stuck to other interests and sharpened my skills and talents.

During college years, I began to focus on giving back and serving the Lord. I wanted to make a difference. I invested my time and energy into the youth group that I had once been a part of and eventually found myself in a leadership role. Later, I took a position as a youth pastor. I was extremely happy and very satisfied ministering to the younger generation.

During this time, I noticed a really nice young woman who also had grown up in our church. She was close friends with my sister Cheryl, and although she was at our house all the time, I never gave her the time of day until after my sophomore year of college, when another guy from her school took an interest in her. She had been looking my way for five years, and she was becoming a bit antsy that I would never give her a chance. Five years is a long time to wait for someone to notice you. She spent her high school prom on the arm of another man. Looking back, this was just the nudge I needed to evaluate her and my feelings and see how special she was. I wasn't going to miss out on what God was giving me.

Becca loved and knew the Lord as well, a beautiful heart wrapped in a beautiful package. I finally opened my eyes and noticed how attractive she actually was. We began dating in the summer of 1997, between my sophomore and junior year of college, a short time before she left to go on a mission trip to Mexico City. I was thrilled to meet somebody who not only matched my interests in faith and art but who was also down to earth and who embraced the simple life I was living. At the time, I was attending a branch of Penn State University, but I was forced to finish my education at the main campus. Although it was very difficult, we enjoyed being a couple via a long-distance relationship. I made it a point to go home and see her every weekend of my junior and senior years. I never missed a single one.

About this time, I began writing poetry and described different life events this way, which was far easier for me than simply writing down events. I was discovering the powerful tool of writing. This was my first encounter with the craft, and I was getting my feet wet. The creative tool of writing allowed me to express what I felt inside more easily than any other avenue.

Poem: November 16, 1998

In the eye of the beholder
What are the eyes?
Their function, their beauty,
What reason do they serve?
To look into the eye,
What does one discover?
What truth does one find?
What treasure is dwelling there . . .
Hidden within?

The eye
A jewel

A sparkling, precious thing
The beauty and fairness of the body
The brightness of the face
The attraction of another's look
The target of a lover's gaze
A window to the soul.

A window?
A transparent glass indeed
This clear glass so perfect,
That the beholder's look perceives inward
To see what secrets lie there
To see what lies upon the heart
The eye is a window to the deepest places
And once looked into,
Nothing can be hidden
The truth is shown through this window
The secrets of one's soul
The desires of one's mind and heart
These eyes . . .
Are treasure keepers
Guards keeping precious objects captive
Waiting . . .
For someone willing to look deep
Deep
Deep
Into the eyes.

(Written after looking into Becca's eyes for the first time
and seeing myself there).

Our relationship quickly became serious. We
knew we were meant to be together. We let the Lord
build our relationship and allowed him to direct our

paths. We even began reading Scripture together and praying together. We were about two hours and thirty minutes apart by car, and I hated being away from her. We emailed each other and sometimes called, but at the time, we were both dead broke and didn't have much money for long-distance calls. The golden age of cell phones had not yet begun.

In my opinion, the old-fashioned way of actually writing words on paper served as a wonderful way to express our love. We wrote to each other constantly, often stylizing letters with artwork, and one of my favorite pastimes was walking to the mailbox common area from my college apartment. I enjoyed receiving mail from someone I loved, and we passed time sharing thoughts back and forth as the year continued. I switched majors part way through my education, so school was strenuous, and I really had to apply myself. This, however, did not change the fact that my thoughts were often in other places. We both admitted that sitting in class, our minds were often elsewhere and easily distracted by daydreams of one another. One time in particular, I wrote my thoughts.

Poem: February 25, 1999

Staring through a window,
I look out into the world, the sky.
My heart then saddens,
Realizing that my love is not found here.
She is in another place,
Far away.
Gazing out another window,

She abides here only in my heart,
My memories,
Promises spoken of
And in photos behind clear glass.
Aching, my heart gapes,
As I think of my love, my precious one.
Thinking of times spent with her,
Hoping she is aching as well . . .
Aching for me,
As she thinks of our future,
Of our togetherness.

Not one here could ever replace her.
Not one could fill the spot she owns in my being.
None among the many could compare to her.
For she is part of me, the one I've been given,
And I long for that part to be with me again.

I desperately want to escape from here,
And go to my love, also behind a window.
I know she longs for me.
To hear my voice,
To look into my eyes,
To feel my touch, my kiss,
To hear the words I long to say.
I want to rush to where my love's name dwells.
To take her hand,
To help her climb out from behind her window.
To flee from the distance that separates us.
The great ocean span I so often wished to cross
Ready to be molded, melted
And made into one flesh and person.
To be with my love, forever together,
Held together by my loving God's own hand.

(Written at Penn State while Becca was at Hempfield High School)

Yes, we were supposed to be studying. It was a huge struggle to pay attention in class some days—especially for a creative, right-brained guy—when your love is so far away. We were engaged the summer between my junior and senior year. She was the first girl I ever kissed, and we never looked back.

We were married in June 2000, on the hottest day of the summer. Sweat trickled down my spine, a combination of nerves and the temperature, as I waited for my bride. The church was packed with family and friends. It seemed as if the whole world wanted to celebrate with us.

Yes, life was good, but married life was even better. She was a tremendous friend and spouse. We had two beautiful boys, Bradley and Justin, and the joy I held in my heart each day as a husband and dad was overwhelming. I was the official entertainment committee each night when I got home from work as two boys ran to the door to greet me. I checked in for duty, giving mom a break. Laughter, love, and smiles filled our home. Life couldn't have been any better.

Where did I think I was going? What did I feel my life would be? I thought it was nothing short of the cotton-cloud daydream of perfection.

Blessed is the man
who walks not in the counsel of the wicked,

nor stands in the way of sinners,
nor sits in the seat of scoffers;
but his delight is in the law of the Lord,
and on his law he meditates day and night.
He is like a tree
planted by streams of water
that yields its fruit in its season,
and its leaf does not wither.
In all that he does, he prospers.
The wicked are not so,
but are like chaff that the wind drives away.
Therefore the wicked will not stand in the
judgment,
nor sinners in the congregation of the righteous;
for the Lord knows the way of the righteous,
but the way of the wicked will perish. (Psalm 1)

Psalm 1 was a very fitting snapshot of what my life looked like at the time. Life was wonderful, and God himself was holding my hand. In a nutshell, I was the poster boy of our local church, a product of what the church could raise up and produce. My wife and I became the poster couple for the church, a spotlight on how God could bring a man and a woman together from the same church body and unite their hearts in marriage. I believe we were the first couple our new pastor married.

I had a steady job as a dairy farmer, I enjoyed my work, and my wife supported me. We had two beautiful, healthy boys. Ministry was rolling. God was using us to do great things in our community, in the lives of those he led to us. The youth group was developing alongside my growing young family. The young people could see a pattern in us, the life that they also wanted to aim for.

Life was exactly like the meadow I illustrated in the beginning of this chapter. The poetic free-flowing verses of life were under my every step. Everything would be just fine and dandy. My favorite Bible verse had become Psalm 34:8. "Taste and see that the Lord is good," and oh man, did I taste! More than tasting for myself, I was convincing others around me to taste as well. Actually, we not only tasted, we devoured—we feasted! I was living proof of Psalm 138:8 in that the Lord had "perfected that which concerneth me" (KJV). Life was not only good, it was surreal.

I didn't know how, but I actually expected life to only get better. Never once did I think anything less. I was living the dream of what every man would want. I expected God to just continue doing what he had done so well from the start. I had a beautiful wife and family and a life full of purpose ahead of me.

Similarly, the book of Job also illustrates the beautiful scene of what my land (life) looked like before the plague came. On so many levels, this was exactly how I felt and looked. I, like Job, was a humble and righteous man, one of character and rich in blessings. Like him, I was just living in the blessings the Lord had given me and was not haughty or prideful. We were enjoying the green meadow for what it was and were very thankful for it.

"There was a man in the land of Uz whose name was Job, and that man was blameless and upright, one who feared God and turned away from evil. There were born to him seven sons and three daughters. He possessed

7,000 sheep, 3,000 camels, 500 yoke of oxen, and 500 female donkeys, and very many servants, so that this man was the greatest of all the people of the east" (Job 1:1–3).

My situation was also like Joseph's, who was loved so greatly by his father that he was given the coat of many colors to wear. He was highly favored, well taken care of, and given special blessings.

"Now Israel loved Joseph more than any other of his sons, because he was the son of his old age. And he made him a robe of many colors" (Genesis 37:3).

Although I was young, I felt incredibly close to the Lord. I was so in tune with the Lord and he with me. It felt as if I, like Joseph, were clothed in his sunshine, colors, and peace. In a sense, I felt as if I wore the coat of many colors my heavenly Father had given me. His banner was over me was love. What could possibly happen or go wrong? God was using me and using us. A rainbow danced over our lives. I was happy and content serving God in this capacity.

My wife and I were making a difference in the lives of others, especially the teenagers in the youth group. Wouldn't God continue this sunny summer daydream and keep using us? Didn't that make sense? Weren't other people being blessed around us? We really were living a dream. Certainly, God would keep our lives going like this. Surely, he was pleased and wanted to bless all that we were doing. All we knew to do was keep walking, keep obeying, and keep pressing into our God.

I tried not to think about it, but one day in our

lives in particular would never be forgotten and would be etched in my mind forever, a turning point. I've tried many times to look back to come up with or find another explanation as to why all the craziness started. I have found none. I've looked into the mirror, asking myself many times if there was another way to see things, another answer, or another reason.

But looking back and contemplating our history so many times, I've never been able to come up with anything different. As hard as I try to make sense of it all, this is the pivotal point that had something to do with it. It was key. It had to be the marker. I often wondered if we would say those words again if we knew what lay ahead of us. One might say it was coincidental, but I know that nothing takes our God by surprise. I cannot think of any explanation other than that one particular day, that one moment of subjection to our Lord. Over and over again, it burns inside me.

That fateful day started just like every other day. Becca and I got dressed, put on our Sunday best, packed the kids and their stuff, and buckled both boys in their car seats. It was a normal Sunday like all the others before it, nothing different about it. During this specific church service, however, the pastor delivered a message that challenged us both. We could not deny that God was very heavy on us, and we responded to his call. No, angels weren't dancing in the ceiling above the altar steps that day, nor were harps playing while we prayed. I don't even think that anyone prayed with us.

We simply listened to the call we felt tugging at our hearts, walked forward, got on our knees, and very earnestly and honestly laid down our lives before the Lord. Out of our own lips, hearts, and minds, the Lord heard our simple, genuine prayer. Few words were needed. We desired to be used by him—as individuals and as a couple. We wanted our lives to make a difference. We wanted to be vessels. We wanted God to take our lives and do something with them. We asked God to be used.

And that was exactly when everything went horribly and terribly wrong.

Chapter 2:
The Swarm of Locusts Come

The word of the Lord that came to Joel, the son of Pethuel:
An invasion of locusts
Hear this, you elders; give ear, all inhabitants of the land!
Has such a thing happened in your days,
or in the days of your fathers?
Tell your children of it,
and let your children tell their children,
and their children to another generation.
~ Joel 1:1–3

A shockwave resonated through their spines, shivering and rattling the fragile glass bones of their framework. While two lovers held on to hope, a lightning strike—quick, an unexpected sentence of terror—drove from the massive dark sky right through it, splitting and shattering their very foundation. The night's fright could not hold a candle to the raw and exposed test results the doctor brought—impossible, unwarranted, and unappreciated.

A husband and wife cared not to hear the life-altering words, those cursed words of pain, nor the embrace of acceptance the doctor expected and hoped for. A resonating gong of unbelief vibrated through the skeletal cores of their souls. They had no handle to grab hold of, to shield, deflect, or toss those words away from innocent ears, as the words so quick and swift were messengers of panic to their minds. A strangely formed lump dangled like cotton in their throats, their now acid-filled stomachs burned as they were told the rarest of the rare had, for some reason, fallen as their portion and lot.

As if to minimize the severity of what was happening and the unlikely chance of someone coming down with this at her age, a shocked young couple was told that this simply doesn't happen, that nobody gets this. Yet even the lottery winner doubts reality, and it happens regardless. Two young lovers held each other in the tightest of embraces, while the summoned plague of sickness disguised as locusts approached to dine and feast. The sky grew increasingly dark and stormy, yet not with the heaviness of rain. Instead, the winged creatures of pain and affliction blew in, blackening the sky, numerous as the sands of the sea to engulf what they may; the locusts began their savage feast on our souls. How frightful and terribly ugly they appeared! Beaded black eyes of mystery, they cared not what we thought of them. Arriving with one purpose, they came to consume . . . and that they did. May God help us.

§

"Now there was a day when his sons and daughters were eating and drinking wine in their oldest brother's house, and there came a messenger to Job and said, "The oxen were plowing and the donkeys feeding beside them, and the Sabeans fell upon them and took them and struck down the servants with the edge of the sword, and I alone have escaped to tell you" (Job 1:13–15).

In late winter of 2006, Valentine's Day to be exact, my wife and I were out enjoying one another's company without children. I had taken Becca on a dinner date to an old favorite restaurant of ours for some authentic Mexican cuisine. It was very nice to have time together, and the food was excellent. This date ended a little oddly though. Although we both ate the same thing and shared each other's plates, she couldn't hold her food down due to pains in her belly. This was the first prompt that eventually led us to a doctor that put her on acid reflux medications. None of the prescriptions worked. As her stomach problems progressively worsened, the process of trying to figure out what the problem was frustrated us.

Doctors were very kind and helpful but had no concrete answers. The trail of medical advice finally led to performing a CT scan and the discovery of a lump blocking the exit of Becca's stomach. Her stomach was greatly distended and had stretched much larger than normal in an attempt to allow food to pass around a mass blocking its exit. There was no place for her meals to go. The doctor then ordered an endoscope. During the procedure, a small tissue sample was taken for review. The doctor came in the hospital room to explain that the sample was probably lymphoma. We were somewhat at ease after we were told that treatment for this was highly successful and fairly easy to go through and tolerate. He explained that she would be treated and on her way in no time. Just to make sure, though, we would wait for the lab results on the tissue taken from a probe during the procedure.

The next day, we were told that contrary to doctor's prior expectations, the biopsy showed that it was, in fact, adenocarcinoma—stomach cancer. Nobody had an explanation for why or how this happened. Simply put, people her age did not get stomach cancer. Now officially serving as our oncologist, the doctor was so surprised by the results of the testing that he reached out to doctors from Korea, a country with a higher incidence of this type of cancer due to diet.

We knew nothing about stomach cancer. We sat bewildered as the doctor talked to us about it, explaining that it wasn't really a common disease in the United States anymore. The invention of the refrigerator had greatly reduced the incidence to a very minimal percentage of people who still got stomach cancer. On top of that, at my wife's young age, the disease was almost unheard of. Most people who did have stomach cancer suffered from it much later in life. He wasn't quite sure of the course of action he wanted to take and was in conversation with experts abroad. Many prayers went up for wisdom for the whole medical team. We were speechless, stunned, and fearful of the unknowns.

Yes, we were shocked. How does a young couple recover from the intensity of that awful conversation?

There was no way humanly possible for a doctor walk in, hand you this kind of news, and for us to be at peace inside. Although we now knew what we were up against, so many unknowns still remained. How would we treat it? What would we do next? There was no place for us to stand except on the foundation of faith and hope that we had in the Lord and the promises that he had given to us in Scripture. Nothing else seemed suitable. Here is an excerpt from my journal when we first found out the news of Becca's cancer.

Journal entry: June 8, 2006

"Until now, we have lived in the dark. The mystery of how Christ loves the church, or better yet, how Christ loves those who do not even love him back, has been revealed to me (us). I admit that we never would have learned this except through the events that we have lived through today. All the doctor's opinions of what this lump could be were thrown in the trash. We are the 1 percent. We are the "almost unheard of." We are the smallest of fractions that somehow keeps finding us. We are the people who are too young to be dealing with this. The extraordinary bomb was dropped on us today.

"So much is unknown about this whole situation. I (we) are sure of one thing: God is in control. He is in our room and in our hearts. Psalm 147:11 and Exodus 23:25. We are standing on our solid rock. He really is the only thing we have, and I think that this is the stage that God loves to work in. God loves the impossible. It's the best stage he could set. When we rely totally on him, then others see it. God gets the glory."

From the beginning, I can read my own journals and see how much hope and promise I (we) held onto. I was so confident that the Lord would bring us through everything with ease. It wasn't really a doubt or question for either of us. The Lord was our confidence, our strong tower, and our healer. He would certainly bring us through. I was so thankful for each and every answer to prayer through the early hospital days. Although we weren't happy about our situation, we were at least happy that God was using us to touch the people we came in contact with. Hope still blazed in our eyes; we hadn't lost any yet. We knew we were in a horrible place and situation, but the Lord was holding us and doing a great job. We tried to brightly shine our light for Jesus wherever he took us.

After the news about the severity of the cancer, the doctor then told us about the surgery. Surgery was scheduled for the very next day, and we placed ourselves in God's hands. Our surgeon had actually scheduled the operation before even coming to talk to us about it. He said it was imperative to operate right away before the cancer spread any further. This would be the beginning of a long series of surgeries and hospital visits and stays, a journey neither of us wished to walk. It was very difficult, but God's favor was shining in us, no matter what was happening. Our surgeon even allowed me to pray with him before the operation. We felt as if our faith were being put to the test. We would excel and rock this test, this trial of life. We would come out victorious on the other side. We were sure of it. We believed.

"And when they had crossed over, they came to

land at Gennesaret. And when the men of that place recognized him, they sent around to all that region and brought to him all who were sick and implored him that they might only touch the fringe of his garment. And as many as touched it were made well" (Matthew 14:34–36).

> And a great crowd followed him and thronged about him. And there was a woman who had had a discharge of blood for twelve years, and who had suffered much under many physicians, and had spent all that she had, and was no better but rather grew worse. She had heard the reports about Jesus and came up behind him in the crowd and touched his garment. For she said, "If I touch even his garments, I will be made well." And immediately the flow of blood dried up, and she felt in her body that she was healed of her disease. And Jesus, perceiving in himself that power had gone out from him, immediately turned about in the crowd and said, "Who touched my garments?" And his disciples said to him, "You see the crowd pressing around you, and yet you say, 'Who touched me?'" And he looked around to see who had done it. But the woman, knowing what had happened to her, came in fear and trembling and fell down before him and told him the whole truth. And he said to her, "Daughter, your faith has made you well; go in peace, and be healed of your disease. (Mark 5:24–34)

Passages like this were all I had to stand on. My weak and weary legs could firmly plant and be confident on this sure foundation. I read those passages and more. It was clear to me that our trust in the Lord would pull us through. He had healed people back then, and he would heal my wife now. We were confidently trusting in the one who could do all things. This would only be a temporary setback.

Journal entry: June 10, 2006

"It is almost ten o'clock in the morning. The nurse has shown favor to me. I am allowed to stay in the Medical Surgical Unit even after hours. Bec is sleeping. I prayed over her. Matthew chapter 7 has become meat to me. I have asked for bread. Please, Lord, don't give me a stone. The Lord himself said the words, *these* words of his word. He cannot go back on them. I am holding him to what he said. It is the only ground I have to stand on.

"I am asking for bread . . .
    1) Let her incision heal at a rate that will astound the doctors
    2) That all of her cancer is gone
    3) That her pain and suffering decreases to a comfortable level
    4) That she can talk to me and give me a hint of love back
    5) That she does not suffer from pneumonia
    6) That she does not contract any infections at the hospital

"Lord . . . please don't give me a stone!"

Well, the temporary setback ended up being a long string of surgeries, treatments, and other types of medical attention. We never dreamed of the long, crazy ride of medical interventions that would come our way. It was almost constant; each day brought a new set of challenges with it.

Sickness has a shadow that no one wishes to step into. Its cold and pale attire is unwelcome; its wardrobe shunned by all those around. No one wants to embrace the plague of sickness, from a common cold to a life-threatening terminal disease. As humans, we pursue life, health, and wellness of the body, soul, and spirit. Though we seek health, in this fallen world, sickness surrounds us. It is part of our universe. Like it or not, since the fall of mankind, it is a very real part of the world we live in. This particular sickness did not ask us to be welcomed or ushered into our lives. We did not invite it. It was not kind, nor did it show any pleasantries or respect to the one it invaded. My wife had no unhealthy risk factors that made her prone to this disease. It simply came, announced itself with stomach pain and the vomiting of a Valentine's Day couple's dinner. We weren't at odds with each other. She did not ask for it. We were not living in any kind of sin to deserve it.

None of those things mattered. Sickness doesn't care.

Before this, our foundation was very strong, but when lightning struck, we took another huge step of spiritual maturity. We were certainly what one would think of as well-rounded Christians, and we had very solid, strong convictions and beliefs. Although we knew the Bible, I suppose that something like this teaches you how to *really* know it, and we were in his Word daily, searching to grab hold of promises to bring us peace.

In this time, we matured tremendously as Christians and also as a married couple. Our time together as a duo was already valuable. Now, however, our time had become priceless. We were very much in love. We made the best of every opportunity. I spent many nights on a hospital chair beside her. We spent time reading to each other and doing things together that nurtured both our friendship and our relationship as spouses. We turned hospital visits and chemo treatments into dates. Although we weren't happy about our circumstances, we purposed to make the best of what we had. We listened to Christian music, held hands, read, and prayed. These were normal routines at the treatment center on chemo days.

Some people know about sickness while others live it. It is a heavy burden that some are troubled with their whole lives. Sickness is the sticky note or label applied when a person is no longer healthy. Sickness is a stigma placed on the head that covers the whole individual, making one person different from others. Sickness is a place of unfathomable medical expense from modern medical science that is supposed to fix everything and make it all better. Sickness is a place where we pat others on the back with a card or a vase of flowers so we feel better ourselves for being healthy when they are not. Sickness is a place that some people cannot handle as we need extra care and effort to help someone else out. Sickness is not fun; with sickness, however, there is still hope—that breath of precious hope that God can do all things, change all things, and heal all things. With sickness, there is still time—time for God to move. There is hope that God will heal. We had that hope. We were not letting go.

We held onto that hope ever so tightly. We held onto it in our hands, no, we strangled it as we clenched it with a desperate grip throughout the days and nights in the hospital and afterward. To be honest, faith and hope were all we had. The cancer was an invisible enemy we fought against, one we couldn't feel. We couldn't tell if it was there or if it had left. The days and weeks that we spent praying, waiting from one scan to the next, we hoped and prayed with the full intensity of fighting for life. We truly believed the cancer was gone or that God *would* take it, that she would be healed and that our prayers would surely be answered. It was no sweat for the Lord, no biggie for him. We knew it was nothing for him to take this situation and turn it into a glorious moment that could be used to reach the masses. We knew God was on our side.

Deep down inside, everybody wants a fairytale life. Nobody ever wakes up one day at age six and says, "I hope my life is filled with heartache, sickness, disaster, or loss. I want to be someone struck with a terminal illness when I grow up." No, we all look to the rainbow of the dream world to see what we desire. We all wish and hope "to live happily ever after." This has been bred into our culture from day one.

Children's cartoons and movies show the prince and the princess happily in love. Teenage action and adventure fiction often show this as the hero, vampire, or other off-beat character promise a never-ending love to the young girl in high school. Even the dramas that adults seem to gravitate toward have the undeniable silver thread that all stories end on a positive note. Nobody ever looks down through life's filmstrip, expecting the loss of a spouse or a sickness that puts you on the couch for a while. Nobody ever hopes for anything less than the perfect iconic dream. We have grown up expecting it. We are encouraged to reach for it from a young age. After all, it is *supposed* to be that way, right? We expect the fairytale to be true and within our grasp. We live wanting and desiring it. It's bred into our humanity. Yet how many of us actually live out that dream?

So what did I expect of my life now? I expected nothing less than the storybook tale of two souls united by marriage in Christ as vessels of his glory with a world-changing ministry. I fully expected the continuation of what seemed to be a perfectly scripted married life. I expected to be used together, to live ministry together. I fully anticipated growing old and gray together with a houseful of grandchildren running around and asking me for ice cream. (I'm a sucker for ice cream.) My sights were set on the abundant life, and I expected no less.

But day by day, visit by visit, the results were not what we expected. Though we held hope high, reality seemed to clash against each step of faith and word of prayer. CT scans that we knew God would wipe clean of cancer were not clean, and those cursed dots of death remained inside a body, despite our full expectance and trust for the Lord's deliverance. The situation began to weigh on us.

As much as I didn't want to admit it, I became very physically tired. Not only did the mental and emotional demands of our situation require a ton of effort and energy, but the physical requirement was drastically higher than I anticipated. I was not only caring for a sick wife but was also holding two young boys afloat. Thankfully, I had a lot of help during this time: in-laws, church friends, and family. Many people came to watch our kids so that we could focus on trying to get better. A meal ministry kept food on our table so I didn't have to cook as much after coming home from work.

And I still needed to work; we needed the money as a family. I had a job to do. My focus had to be balanced between what I had to do and what I needed to do. There was a big difference. I had to pick and choose what my energy was used for. Some might fault me for not doing one thing or another, but I was and still am only human, and I had to prioritize what I did. I figured if we were taking care of our spiritual side first and family second, then the rest would fall into place. If we didn't get a bath that night or we didn't brush our hair that morning, well, it would just have to be what it was. We needed to apply a lot of grace and leeway.

It was wonderful to have help, but I felt a certain sense of isolation in it all. Though the world came to our side, we still felt alone, trapped inside a closed box. Nobody else really knew what it felt like to be inside that box. Our arms were open wide to the help and encouragement from others, but in the same sense, we felt as if we had lost a certain dignity as we felt we should be able to take care of ourselves.

Inside of a man is the innate nature to provide, protect, and care for his own. I was determined to do that if it killed me. I worked round the clock, doing everything I could to keep the family's wheels spinning. Others began to notice that I was neglecting myself in the process. I foolishly thought that I didn't need to worry about my own condition. I learned the hard way that you need to take care of yourself to take care of others. Still, I burned the candle at both ends.

During this time, some people unknowingly placed pressure on me, which made life much more difficult. Sadly, we began to face and feel as if we were somehow taboo. Some tried to alter our thought patterns. Opinions were dumped in our laps. It started to mess with our minds. After enough of that, we started to question ourselves. Maybe there was a reason we were in this mess, and we might be at fault in some way. After all, isn't that what the Bible says? We just ask in prayer and everything is fine, right?

"Is anyone among you suffering? Let him pray. Is anyone cheerful? Let him sing praise. Is anyone among you sick? Let him call for the elders of the church, and let them pray over him, anointing him with oil in the name of the Lord. And the prayer of faith will save the one who is sick, and the Lord will raise him up. And if he has committed sins, he will be forgiven" (James 5:13–15).

Journal Entry: 2006

"I am rowing a one-man raft to shore. The fog surrounds me. It is morning, and already my arms have failed to strengthen my journey. It is a deep pain . . . one that cannot be fixed by the futile remedies of those who claim to supposedly know or by some professional opinion that simply speaks a Band-Aid into the air. All have failed to do much to keep me rowing. The battle is my own; I know it full well.

"Help has no consequence from the standpoint of outside human aid. It is so easy. Almost too easy. If help had consequences, opinions would be seriously weighed and given only after much thought, debate, prayer, and research. Since these are tossed to the bottom of the water that I row through, a word of help thrown carelessly to me neither propels me or weighs me down. All these gifts do is tag themselves onto a long list of hopeful thoughts that build my confidence for nothing.

"I am used to frustration, as I have rowed day after day for months. Others block my view. They come and row their rafts in circles around me. I have enough trouble rowing, let alone dodging other rafts as they confuse the straight line I follow. How I wish companions would see that I am filtering through the rafts of star-gazers. Throw me a line that helps pull me through!

"And then they vanish. All are gone. Now I am left with the chopped water that tired arms and brain cells must manage through, when simple was the path before they came. And I do see the land! The Lord has cleared the fog and smoke of the morning mist to point the shore to me. Oh, how I see it. It is ever so clear to me. I have etched its path on my heart and mind. My map dwells within me.

"And then the fog closes back in, and the enemy taunts me, threatening to tear the map out of my soul to trample it. He desires it with a relentless pursuit. Day after day, he swirls around my tired head, asking for the map God let me record on fleshly tablets of emotion. My confused mind wonders what is real. Do I really see the shore? Mirages as nightmares make me wonder as terror strikes my mental capacities. Which way was the shore? Or did I ever see it?

"As Job or David, misery sounds this onward flight to a safe location. I wonder how long I can paddle. How long will my sanity remain? Will a land-bound man collapse from the onward push in vain? Will all confidence and determination fall short of the goal at hand? At times, I certainly wonder. Each day, my prayer rises above the fog. Each night, I light a lamp, a humble request. When will the Lord hear me? For how long must I row as a dead man walking? And so, my lips speak out my request once again. O Lord, my only God, you are the only sole help that could bring aid. Nobody else can see or hear the real trouble that I remain in. If this journey is to train me or forge me, refrain me, or refine me, give me the strength I need to complete it.

"When I lay down, let my eyelids find peace and rest. May my arms and mind find relief. God before me . . . I plead with you. If I must continue rowing, may I do so in your wake. Then I will have ease of travel. Then I will undeniably know the way. Then will my enemy have no triumph over me, for you watch me as I pursue you. Fain not to keep me as your own lips have promised. For then would I be a man most miserable. But with you, Oh Lord, is joy and peace."

I feel a certain need to liberate those who have felt this heavy weight from others, as I was one of you. It is unfair and, frankly unbiblical, to impose on a sick person that the failure of healing is derived or decided by their own lack of faith. It is crazy to explain, reason, or justify that sickness is because they are not right with the Lord or due to some other form of misguided human judgment.

Let me ask the average person this question: "Does God answer all your prayers the *exact* way you want him to?" Of course, he doesn't. He is frankly too loving and compassionate to give us what we ask for in our limited understanding. Let me ask another question. Do you condemn yourself when you pray about something for your own personal life and do not end up receiving a yes? If we are honest with ourselves, we will admit that we don't receive a yes to each and every prayer we ask.

Simply put, God doesn't answer each and every prayer the way we want. Sometimes he has something else up his sleeve. If we don't pass judgment on ourselves in our own prayer lives for a different answer than we expected, why do we pass judgment on the sick individual who does not receive what they desire? Nobody heaps a single thought of guilt or judgment on their own prayer. Yet so often, over time, we even forget what we are asking of God. If that is the case, why would any man or woman who is honest with themselves project this kind of burden onto a fellow brother or sister? Why?

We do it because it's easy to do, and it gives us an out. We are no longer held accountable in our own minds for the outcome of the situation. When our prayers for someone aren't answered, sadly some stoop to supposing that the sick person did something wrong and deserves being sick. Sometimes, we suppose that the man, woman, or child has sinned. Sometimes, we suppose that they caused it or that they simply don't have the faith necessary to be healed. At this point, we allow our prayers to now cease, and we no longer make the effort to spend the time talking to God about them. It's not our duty anymore. Sadly and selfishly, we justify ourselves. We are now free to go about our own business, assuming that sometimes prayer is the most taxing and heaviest responsibility on a person.

Phrased in that way, it sounds absurd, but that is exactly what we do. Isn't God in charge anyhow? Can't he deal with making the person right in sinless standing and then heal the person afterward? Well, this type of attitude, in actuality, places the dependency of the miracle on the sick person instead of on God. When we heap this type of burden on a sick person, what we are really doing is saying that the ability to be healed does not lie in the hands of our Father but in the hands of the hurting. Is that right? Is it fair? Certainly not! Is my God's power to heal limited by my faith? If so, then who is really the one in the control?

Is God's creative power and nature dependent on my knowledge and ideas or what I can come up with? Absolutely, positively, 1,000 percent no, no, and no! It sounds silly when we script it like that, but sadly enough, Christians too often place the enormous weight of such thought on sick people, their loved ones, and their caretakers. The power that God has to heal is not dependent at all on little old me. God can create and speak a star into existence in the sky or speak into existence the very life you and I breathe each day. God is not dependent on a person to believe in him to exist. Neither does he need faith in order to heal. God is no more dependent on a human being to justify anything he is or does than I am dependent on Mickey Mouse to justify my own existence. We are not God. Stop transferring power where it does not belong.

Job ran into the same situation. In the midst of terrible hurt, pain, and affliction, his buddies came over to sit with him. What sounds great at first glance proved to be a horrible situation for poor Job. Instead of actually helping the wounded soul, all they did was tell Job it was his own fault. If he truly looked inside, he would find the root cause for all his turmoil. They were searching for the answers as to why poor Job was being run through such a grinder in life. When they couldn't come up with the answers they needed, they pinned it all on the very friend that they came to comfort. It is a mystery still to this day why God allowed the sufferings of Job, but nevertheless, he did.

Job's buddies tried to pass the buck. They falsely reasoned that Job must have sinned and brought this all on himself. I'm tremendously thankful that I don't have any friends named Eliphaz. Look at what he said to poor Job when things got rough: "Remember: who that was innocent ever perished? Or where were the upright cut off? As I have seen, those who plow iniquity and sow trouble reap the same. By the breath of God they perish, and by the blast of his anger they are consumed" (Job 4:7–9).

In other words, Eliphaz was telling Job that he was getting what he deserved. That might sound harsh when stated like that. But many times, even people with the best of intentions can unknowingly say the same thing by simple phrases that sound much different to the sick ear than to their own when they speak. If we only could hear the words our own mouths utter. "Then Job answered and said: 'I have heard many such things; miserable comforters are you all. Shall windy words have an end? Or what provokes you that you answer? I also could speak as you do, if you were in my place; I could join words together against you and shake my head at you. I could strengthen you with my mouth, and the solace of my lips would assuage your pain'" (Job 16:1–5).

"Then Job answered and said:
'How long will you torment me
and break me in pieces with words?
These ten times you have cast reproach upon me;
are you not ashamed to wrong me?'" (Job 19:1–3).

"All my intimate friends abhor me,
and those whom I loved have turned against me.
My bones stick to my skin and to my flesh,
and I have escaped by the skin of my teeth.
Have mercy on me, have mercy on me, O you my friends,
for the hand of God has touched me!
Why do you, like God, pursue me?
Why are you not satisfied with my flesh?" (Job 19:19–22).

Unfortunately, this type of thing happens all the time. It happened to me. It happened to other people that I know. Again, I reiterate, that even people with the best of intentions don't know how hurtful simple clichés sound to the person entrenched in the battle. "Just believe," people will tell you. "You've got to have faith!" Isn't this what the Bible tells us in the first place? "And he said to her, 'Daughter, your faith has made you well; go in peace, and be healed of your disease'" (Mark 5:34).

Jesus himself tells us to have faith. "And Jesus said to him, 'If you can! All things are possible for one who believes.'" (Mark 9:23).

So isn't believing enough, in and of itself? Others might insinuate that the sick must not doubt God's power to heal. Others boldly say you must "claim your healing in faith." Seriously? Claim? Who are we to tell the Lord what we deserve? Do we, as humans, deserve anything from God Almighty that we should have the audacity to claim something from him? The damaging effects of this kind of teaching can immensely hurt the sick individual even when the friend is trying to help. In my wife's situation, did I believe for her healing? Yes, yes, a thousand times, yes! I read every Scripture there was to read. I looked at all the healing miracles Christ did in the Gospels. I dwelled on those passages and ruminated long and hard on Scripture and stood on them as my foundation. I thought about all those things. I had faith.

Journal entry: February 6, 2008

"I am afraid to speak my thoughts. I do not want to invite problems. I am in anguish right now, but I am afraid to write about it and am wiser. At least, I think I shouldn't talk to Bec about it. I am in anguish inside. I finished Psalm 119. What do I do? Where do I turn? I feel alone.

Wondering and searching to hear 'good job,' 'well done,' or 'I'm proud.' I keep searching. I am just about deflated. Can I speak my mind?

"A phone call to [someone to help] was just the thing I needed. She said I have to be a real person. She said people try to find something to blame to help them feel better. She said it's not my fault and I don't have to kill myself trying to be a super Christian in this situation. She said to take what others say with a grain of salt. People, even Christians, even [people in the church] say things that will really put pressure on me. Guess what? I can't do anything. It's God. It's a shame that people put pressure on you that you have to take it and deal with it. She said (after I did) that Psalm 119 was so special to her too. She agrees with me that it is ridiculous to expect people to be superman. David poured his heart out. We are biblically allowed to do the same. God wants our hearts. Real prayers. Real people. To back this up, we were reading Psalm 40 tonight. Verse 6 says, "Sacrifice and offering thou didst not desire; mine ears hast thou opened: burnt offering and sin offering hast thou not required" (KJV).

"God doesn't want us to stand and dance on our heads and do all kinds of goofy things for Bec's healing. All he wants is our hearts. That is so wonderful! God is so good. I told this to Bec as we read it. I don't want her to feel trapped in guilt or pressure either."

Journal entry: February 7, 2008

"Psalm 44:9–16. This section, read by the person trapped

55

in the guilt and pressure faced to be a so-called super Christian can be medicine to the soul. David was real. God didn't strike him down, punish him, or make him feel guilty with negative feelings. God realizes who we are and how he made us. He knows we have questions and feelings of abandonment. After all, only God can see what is happening and when it is happening and what he is doing. He doesn't expect us to know. We are human. To not feel these things would be outside normal human nature that God intended for us. The pressure that other Christians either knowingly or unknowingly put on us is *unbiblical*."

"Yes, I certainly did believe, and when a person genuinely believes God can and will heal them or a loved one but it doesn't happen, the weight of that is hugely devastating to an individual. If we truly want to help the hurting soul, we need to jump in the trenches with them and *identify* with their affliction. Understandably, this person is not being healed for a certain reason, but in reality, it may have *absolutely nothing to do with them*. Jesus's disciples had this very thought one day. They even asked their master about it. Jesus had a perfect answer to explain the situation.

"As he passed by, he saw a man blind from birth. And his disciples asked him, 'Rabbi, who sinned, this man or his parents, that he was born blind?' Jesus answered, 'It was not that this man sinned, or his parents, but that the works of God might be displayed in him. We must work the works of him who sent me while it is day; night is coming, when no one can work. As long as I am in the world, I am the light of the world'" (John 9:1–5).

I have often thought in hindsight of the perfect reply to those who heap rocks of burden on the backs of others in this situation. "Well, if all it takes is faith, then use *your* faith to heal me. Maybe I'm not being healed because *you* don't have enough faith!"

> While he was still speaking, someone from the ruler's house came and said, "Your daughter is dead; do not trouble the Teacher anymore." But Jesus on hearing this answered him, "Do not fear; only believe, and she will be well." And when he came to the house, he allowed no one to enter with him, except Peter and John and James, and the father and mother of the child. And all were weeping and mourning for her, but he said, "Do not weep, for she is not dead but sleeping." And they laughed at him, knowing that she was dead. But taking her by the hand he called, saying, "Child, arise." And her spirit returned, and she got up at once. And he directed that something should be given her to eat. And her parents were amazed, but he charged them to tell no one what had happened. (Luke 8:49–56)

Did the people in this passage have faith? Nope. In fact, they laughed in Christ's face. Did Jesus still heal her? Yep. Fascinating, isn't it?

I know that personally, if other people I've prayed for could be healed just because of *my* faith, they would have been healed *long* ago. I have prayed for other brothers and sisters in Christ for a very long time. I've prayed for the healing of unsaved people too. Some, sadly, are never released from this burden of sickness.

Does that mean that God didn't hear my prayers? Theirs? Is the physical restoration in the exact way I desire the only evidence that the Lord hears my words to him? Of course not.

Therefore in the same way, we see that faith alone is not the secret formula. There is more to it than that. Let me propose another question: Would you tell the apostle Paul that he didn't have enough faith? I highly doubt any of us would nor will we tell him that when we meet him face to face one day. He was a man with tremendous faith. He was used to heal the needs of many people in very mysterious ways: "And God was doing extraordinary miracles by the hands of Paul, so that even handkerchiefs or aprons that had touched his skin were carried away to the sick, and their diseases left them and the evil spirits came out of them" (Acts 19:11–12).

Does that sound like the description of a man without faith? On the contrary, he had a steadfast faith and focus on the Lord, so much so that he couldn't wait to pass from this life to the next just to be with him. He was a rock-solid man of faith, a man of dignified character. If anybody could be healed by faith alone, one would say it was the apostle Paul. In fact, Paul asks for something of the Lord; he asked the Lord to take the thorn from his side three times.

So to keep me from becoming conceited because of the surpassing greatness of the revelations, a thorn was given me in the flesh, a messenger of Satan to harass me, to keep me from becoming conceited. Three times I pleaded with the Lord about this, that it should leave me. But he said to me, "My grace is sufficient for you, for my power is made perfect in weakness." Therefore I will boast all the more gladly of my weaknesses, so that the power of Christ may rest upon me. For the sake of Christ, then, I am content with weaknesses, insults, hardships, persecutions, and calamities. For when I am weak, then I am strong. (2 Corinthians 12:7–10)

If Paul, a righteous man of God, was not healed because God had allowed purpose to enter his life, who are we to say that a healing is the *only* evidence that God can hear our feeble prayers to him? A healing or answer that we desire is not an indicator of God listening to us in the least. The person with the strongest of faith, the most spiritually right person who is in-tune with God, can ask healing from the Lord, only to be told "I have a much better plan for you." Therefore, we as Christians cannot and should not place guilt, judgment, or condemnation on others who are desperately pleading with Christ for healing but don't receive it. It is not our place to judge. We are not God.

In my opinion, a much more effective approach would be to sympathize with an individual on their level, praying *with* them instead of just *for* them. Is there a better way to be a friend to the hurting and afflicted brother or sister? Absolutely! Job himself reveals it in a response to his friends.

"Even now, behold, my witness is in heaven,
and he who testifies for me is on high.
My friends scorn me;
my eye pours out tears to God,

that he would argue the case of a man with God,
as a son of man does with his neighbor" (Job 16:19–21).

How can you help that afflicted friend of yours? Jump or dive right in with them. Roll up your sleeves and don't be afraid to get messy. Identify with them. Stand beside them, not above them, and plead alongside with them to the throne of grace. It may be that the Lord answers these prayers with deliverance. If not, you have only been a hand of encouragement and edification, helping strengthen, mature, and build up your brother or sister in Christ. Be in the battle with them. Let your lips "argue the case of a man with God." Let your knees be calloused from kneeling in prayer with that individual. Don't just pray for them. Remember, sometimes Jesus healed even those that didn't ask for a healing to begin with.

On another note of pain, I feel a certain sadness in my heart for those sheep that have been "fleeced" by a shepherd. This is an incredibly delicate subject, but I want to address it as I also feel the need to liberate those that have been negatively affected by so-called faith healers.

Do not get me wrong. Genuine people have laid hands on the sick, and they have recovered. It is one of the gifts God's Holy Spirit gives to the body of Christ, a necessary part of a healthy church, and a necessary part of the advancement of God's kingdom. "Now you are the body of Christ and individually members of it. And God has appointed in the church first apostles, second prophets, third teachers, then miracles, then gifts of healing, helping, administrating, and various kinds of tongues. Are all apostles? Are all prophets? Are all teachers? Do all work miracles? Do all possess gifts of healing? Do all speak with tongues? Do all interpret? But earnestly desire the higher gifts" (1 Corinthians 12:27–31).

In the history of Christ's church, God's Spirit has worked through some people by the gift of healing. People have laid hands on the sick, and others have walked away whole. No doubt, the Spirit can heal. The problem arises when a man or woman who is not given this gift takes advantage of innocent folks that are in desperate need of healing and who speak empty words of promises with no backing. Let me explain.

One night, my wife and I attended a so-called healing service that was located quite a distance away from our small country town at a big city church. After making the trip there, I walked in, noticing how different it was from the hometown scene. It was a very fancy place, unlike any church I had ever attended. At this point, my wife was already very frail. We had been trusting and praying for a miracle and continued day and night in prayer that we would receive one. Word was passed on to us about this healing service. In innocence and good intentions, people wanted to see her healed and restored. We were slightly skeptical but hopeful and made the trip anyhow as we desperately wanted her free from this disease.

When the supposed healer began his segment of the service, a few immediate red flags stood out. I had never seen a pastor or preacher so well dressed. His shoes were gleaming and shining, perfectly polished. His suit was expensive-looking. His hair was styled unlike anyone I've ever seen stand in a pulpit. Red flags aside, I decided to commit to the service because I figured *God*—not a mere man—would heal my wife.

Since then, I've thought a lot about that night. Looking back, I suppose that she was an easy target. Anybody with eyes could see that she was sick. Unfortunately, instead of just receiving prayer and the laying on of hands as Scripture instructs us, she was put on a pedestal to become a spectacle for all to see. She was called out and made an example. She was boldly prayed over with convincing and powerful words, as if a man's voice or intonation could bring change. On the contrary, I fully know that my God can heal even if I don't say a single word. No, the sound of a man's voice or the words actually said matters not. God looks at the heart. I knew this full well, yet I stayed by her side as we hoped for a miracle, even here.

At this stage of the cancer progression, she no longer had a uterus. It had been removed when the cancer invaded surrounding organs. This was by far the hardest surgery on her emotionally, as she felt a lack of dignity and loss of self-esteem and even womanhood. We still hoped for and desired more children once she was healthy and on her feet, so it seemed as if this surgery crushed our dreams. We were already blessed with two wonderful boys, but deep down, we were hoping more would follow. The hysterectomy was a low blow to both our future dreams and my wife's feeling of femininity. Somehow or another, during the course of this man's ranting and raving and carrying on, he learned that in her current situation, she could no longer have children. And so he prayed. He prayed louder. He prayed with intensity and drama. He claimed she was healed. He claimed she had a victory. He claimed that her body was whole.

In faith, did we believe it? I didn't believe that mere man without God's power could heal any more than Big Bird from Sesame Street could. Did I believe that the God of the entire universe could make my wife whole when we trusted and obeyed his every step? Yes. Emphatically yes.

At that very moment, the entire church erupted in raging applause for my wife. The cheer of a crowd who also desired a healing like the one they had just witnessed in her shouted to the rooftops. We were smiling and thrilled. We honestly believed it was true. Then, the atmosphere oddly shifted. A microphone was shoved in my face as I was asked how I felt. Although I was uncomfortable about how she was called out and made a spectacle of, I thought for a second and then replied. "I feel like going home and making a baby."

Looking back, I suppose I probably shouldn't have spoken my mind so openly. Some people there might not have taken what I said the way it sounded in my own mind. But it was the truth. We wanted more children. If the Lord had, in fact, fully healed her, then I wanted to go home and get right to it. We had three more children to bring into the world, as we wanted five, and if God had healed her, well, we'd better get started tonight.

Almost as soon as the words came out of my mouth, I saw what had actually occurred. Forgive me of my cynicism, but in hindsight, I could see how truly clever this man was. This woman, my wife, clearly sick and frail, was randomly selected from the crowd. Her condition was no secret. A stranger in a crowd of a thousand could have guessed that she had cancer. It certainly didn't take Einstein to figure it out. Then, after she was made the center of a huge show, no one in the audience could know that she was *not* healed, not even me, not even herself. You cannot feel cancer, so you cannot feel its absence or feel it leave.

It had invaded her body unnoticed a long time ago. She didn't even know it was there for months and possibly years. When the man on stage said she was healed, well, who would say that she was not? Furthermore, she would have been a perfect pick to stand before the crowd since we were a young, loving couple. She gripped the hearts of the people there just like she gripped the hearts of people everywhere else she went. Sadly, with her supposed healing, the next thing this man talked about was money. Stunned, I watched as checkbooks immediately came out all over the room. I was appalled, simply shook to the core.

I could not believe that right after my wife and I were put on a platform for everyone to see, the very next thing spoken about was the amount of money everybody had in their pockets. My belly erupted like a bowl of hot acid. I was more than upset; I was disgusted. When it was clear that the fleecing of the flock had begun, I couldn't take it, and we decided to leave. Sadly, we walked out of the church with our tails between our legs and our dignity in our hands. A horrible feeling swept over me. What was done was done. Nothing could be changed. We went home with heavy hearts. Still believing for a miracle from

God, we hoped that he had heard our desperate cry, an innocent and naive one, even in the midst of such a show and disgrace to his holy name.

The next scan showed that the preacher man's words were nothing more than fluff. Our hopes and prayers were still not answered, despite our honest belief, although the supposed healer's pockets jingled with a bit more change. We were very discouraged. Holding onto what little hope we had, we knew God still had time. We stood strong, knowing that God could still move, heal, and help us in this situation. We also knew what happened back in that church was very unfortunate, at least in our eyes. We were certainly ashamed. I wonder how much money came in that night because of us. I suppose that the place could have been made even fancier or he could have afforded another thousand-dollar suit. We were innocent, and so were those who accompanied us. We were there in integrity and honesty, desperately reaching out to the Lord of healing. Why we were still lacking, God only knows.

In addition to being an author, I also call myself an artist. Some of the artwork that God has done through me has floated around the globe a bit. In art, one has to develop the lights and darks of a painting at the same time. Without one, you cannot appreciate the other. Without a dark, you don't realize how bright the lights are. If a painting is simply all bright, it loses the dynamics and contrast.

Certain joys in life are not fully understood without the presence of a few hard moments that enhance them. With these present hardships, our relationship only forged stronger and brighter. True, it was tremendously difficult to go through these challenges, but we were totally rocking it, and our love and marriage only became stronger. Our love overflowed, which could be seen everywhere we went. Hardships fused us closer together as a couple. For example, others came up to us, telling us how nice it was to see a couple holding hands as they walked into the grocery store. Nurses commented that they wanted to have a love like we did. Many nurses' eyes leaked with tears as they felt it was so unfortunate that we were in such a battle. We didn't necessarily realize that it was happening, but we became an example of what Christian love in marriage should look like. It blazed like a torch in the darkest night.

Over time, my wife's body became weaker and weaker. Though we still clung to the Lord (and to each other) with everything we had, we both grew weary. She was really becoming thin, and her energy was depleting rapidly. During these weeks and months, she may have been diminishing physically, but she was still a lighthouse of hope and an example of faith in the dark night sky. Her faith and strength in the Lord were evident to all who saw her. While we were wearing out physically, God was still there with us. He held us every day. We were being used unlike any other time in our lives. We were the strongest in faith we had ever been. Even though God had us in his hands, the body has limits, and we began to reach those.

Journal entry: July 7, 2006

"The acid test of our faith is our obedience."

~ Charles Stanley[1]

"I am just about at the end of what a tired man can endure. The trials that I've faced over the last couple hours/days are sure a test of my character and maturity. If I've not seen enough yet . . . a bucket of ordeals has been dumped on my head. What am I to think? What does God desire of me? What does he want? The calling on my life is ever so evident now. I have realized that I am not an ordinary person. How could I be? God is obviously pursuing me with a relentless pull to push me deeper into a faith that knows no failure and no regrets."

Well, my wife and I were tested indeed. Our faith and our hope were put to the test for two full years. The admittance in and out of hospitals, combined with the chemotherapy, surgeries, trying to keep a job as a dairy farmer, and raising two little boys was extremely taxing and difficult. The boys wanted time. They needed a dad. My wife needed care. Our relationship needed some date nights as well to keep it healthy. I still needed to work and hold down a job. We all had to eat supper. Kids needed doctor checkups and dentist visits. Our ministry at the church was very much still alive and needed our attention. Everything needed to be done at once, and I was worn out. It was a very pressing time.

Over and over in my journal, I wrote about it, and now I can look back on entries that started out with, "I thought I was tired before." In all reality, it was only the beginning of a fifteen-year marathon I would need to learn to manage. I didn't know it then, but many of the early physical struggles were nothing compared to the crises that came later in life. Nothing would be easy from now on. Looking back, I didn't know how straightforward those early struggles were. I didn't know that what I was dealing with now was a lot simpler than what would come later. In some ways, I was going through early preparation and gym training sessions. The next years of my life would be an ironman triathlon that I never dreamed or thought possible. I never expected things to get any worse. Surely God would come to the rescue as I believed him each step of the way. Surely he would heal. Two little boys were counting on it. I was counting on it. A church was counting on it. A world watched.

Surely the stage was set for an incredible miracle of God.

I believed.

Chapter 3
The Swarm Devours

What the cutting locust left,
the swarming locust has eaten.
What the swarming locust left,
the hopping locust has eaten,
and what the hopping locust left,
the destroying locust has eaten.
~ Joel 1:4

Tis better to have loved and lost
than never to have loved at all.
~ St. Augustine

Journal entry in memory of Becca:

"I can't help it. It doesn't seem right. She was beautiful, beloved by her people, treasured by her husband. They were perfect for each other. Yet cancer swept her away. She shone like a star to the people who looked up to her. She chose to burn brightly despite her illness."

"While he was yet speaking, there came another and said, 'The fire of God fell from heaven and burned up the sheep and the servants and consumed them, and I alone have escaped to tell you'" (Job 1:16).

I held two boys who could not hold themselves as a faint reality of what was occurring only brushed their backside to alarm them of its presence. Quite possibly, my arms held those boys, not only to hold them up but as a brace for myself. I hoped the strength I wrapped around them would wrap around me as well. Two young faces knew that mourning was appropriate, but they couldn't fully understand or fathom what they really mourned. They leaned against the dark black fabric of the suit I hoped never to wear, the tie that I never wanted to place around my neck again. I held them.

It was no secret to anyone present, as everyone there could clearly see that I was really the one needing to be held. And they had that moment. The one no small boy should ever have to face or live through. The moment that no boy can take in or process or determine if it is fair or real or unimaginable. My boys, at ages five and three, were forced to look it square in the eye and accept the moment that they would have to say goodbye to Mom for the last and final time until we would all meet again in heaven.

And it crushed me inside.

I kissed the smooth mahogany wood grains of her casket. My lips released their seal, hoping to hang on forever, and I stood over the closed encasement that kept me from seeing her anymore. "Take all the time you need

. . . " That permission, those words broke through the concrete levy holding back my composure and dignity. My shield now down, broken, I was left bare, naked, exposed, and vulnerable to the world. My face collapsed once more in a second embrace, altogether far less composed. I wept, emotions no longer held neatly or in check. I sobbed over her.

Clean, mirrored perfections, previously untouched, now were marred with tears, the running of my nose, fingerprints, and steam from my breath. "Take your time," I was told. The words reminded me of the fact I wished not to accept. I knew that this was the very last time I would have any touch, any tangible reality of the one I was burying. I sobbed uncontrollably, in the presence of whoever was there to witness my tears. It did not matter. I didn't care. And I would be more undignified than this, for the love of my life is departing from my grasp.

That, in a nutshell, would be the umbrella of consolation I would try to cover my face with. Though the eyes of others witnessed this moment, raw and unrehearsed, it was only truly seen and understood between me and the one I loved. She was the only one I meant or intended to communicate anything to. The world blacked out and rightly so. Nobody else was present in that moment. I spoke to my wife, only for her and God's ears to hear. A sacred phrase, once spoken, with everything I had within me. Our last words. And in death, we finally did, unfortunately, part.

"The death of a beloved is an amputation."
~ C. S. Lewis[2]

And death attempted to part us, though I often fought it. For as the days ticked by in the undulating pendulum tap of time, a numbed mind and weary soul went to visit a buried wife each and every day. I desperately tried to convince myself that "death cannot part us" as I continued my routine. Yet the days proved otherwise as my efforts slowly slipped into the inevitable reality of loss. The warm sunshine kept me comfortable as I lay there in the grass at her gravesite where we frequently had picnics and ice cream dates together. An ice cream shop, a local favorite spot, was right across the road, and so the boys and I often took our moose tracks, birthday cake, orange dreamsicle, or cookie dough cones to go and spend time with Mom on the grassy hillside where she rested.

Many summer suns dipped over the western horizon to my backside as I lay beside the one I longed to never leave, facing her, hoping to keep her alive, hoping to share a continued life with her. I was daring to still keep the passion we once waved across the sky for others to see and look to and hope in.

In time, autumn leaves changed the scene, and colored mums were planted in a vain effort to make her place cozier, as if she were even there anyway. Yet I planted and cared. Time passed, and so did the sights and sounds. The peace and intimacy that enveloped the location, making it almost sacred as the seasons changed before me helped me process. I have many memories of what we did there, things done with Mom. A beautiful majestic whitetail rack of eight points held his head high to appreciate the moment she and I were sharing. The buck was unafraid, seemingly paying homage to the sacred grounds. He stood tall, saluting before moving on. Several times, we brought sleds to include mom in the fun that we all wished she could share with us. She was the very last gravesite occupied, on the very outer edge of the cemetery with a nice long hill underneath her, perfect for sledding. Others must have thought we were crazy.

"What we have once enjoyed deeply we can never lose.
All that we love deeply becomes a part of us."
~ Helen Keller[3]

"They live forever in your broken heart that doesn't seal back up. And you come through. It's like having a broken leg that never heals perfectly—that still hurts when the weather gets cold, but you learn to dance with the limp."
~ Anne Lamott[4]

We desperately tried to keep Mom involved in everything we did. We stopped at the cemetery for special moments with her for holidays and birthdays. We stopped by to tell her when special occasions had occurred or for important milestones in our lives. We didn't want her to miss out on the wonderful moments that came our way, and we had much to include her in. After vacations, we brought seashells to show her and leave by her gravestone. We even took her silly gifts like birthday treats, although we knew she couldn't eat them. The fact of the matter, the one thing we so earnestly didn't want to believe, was that Mom wasn't there. She was doing much better things in heaven instead of sled riding in the cold. I'm no cold weather fan; I'll be so glad to get to heaven and not see snow anymore (author smiles ear to ear).

Grief is a mystery. The way that the human mind handles grief is a profound riddle that still lies in wait to be understood by even the best and most intelligent among us. Unique to each one it encounters, it puts on a different disguise each time. I suppose no two people grieve exactly the same way.

I knew Grief. I capitalize that as a proper noun, because Grief is an entity. Grief is an identity. It is a foe that if you do not at least voluntarily and temporarily dance with and surrender to, even for a short time, it will turn around and bite you hard with a venomous sting. All who go through loss must go on this journey and face it to one degree or another. It is a land of various phases, a place that changes as time progresses. The love of my life had passed from this world to the next, and I was left here to hold all the pieces and try to put them back together again.

Losing a spouse is incredibly hard. My heart feels compassion and sympathy for all who have ever lost a loved one: a parent, a sibling, a child, or a friend. All these losses are extremely hard. For me, losing a spouse presented significant difficulties in many situations. I am not downplaying the grief that anyone out there is facing. But what I am saying is that in every other situation of death, one can cling to a spouse for support and encouragement. When your spouse is the one who passes, you have nobody to turn to. You face a severing, a discarding of the other half of your soul and body, leaving you unable to function for all intents and purposes.

When you have been married for a while, the bond and relationship that you form with your spouse leaves you dependent on that person. You share workloads, you calm each other emotionally, you pray for one another, you support each other in dreams and wishes, you can be there to push one another forward, and you can hold onto each other when you need to cry. I did not have any of those luxuries. I felt as if I were ripped in half, forced to continue functioning with only one arm and one leg. My sweetie was my other half, and now, she was on the other side of heaven.

From what I understand, men also experience different emotions from women in this type of loss. Someone once told me that if a man were out floating on the ocean and a life raft came by with only room for one, he would heave his wife to safety without a single thought. But women don't think that way. They are wired to sacrifice and primarily care for those who have passed through their own bowels. If a woman were in that same situation, she would most likely heave her child to safety. Although we would never hope to be in this rhetorical dilemma, women feel that their children are irreplaceable while men feel their wives are. Neither is wrong or right; it's just the way we are wired.

Job dealt with death as well. In Job 1:16, cited earlier in this chapter, he lost all of his children. How can a man bear something like that? For one to say that nobody can understand what you are going through is a strong fallacy. It may seem that way when you are suffering from grief, but actually, many people in the world may be in the exact same situation as you are. If you look, you will find someone. In the Bible, Job lost almost everything he had. All his children were stripped away from him. Death was all around.

"Not only is death inevitable; death is necessary for us to inherit the new life we are to enjoy in Christ."
~ Max Lucado[5]

Death forces you to look at things differently. You cannot survive the death of a close loved one and not have your perspective changed. For positive or negative, you will have a new view that will never be the same again. Grieving for me is and was different from the next man. I had to do what I needed to help myself.

Although it would seem odd to some, I needed to trace the path of doctors and visit the hospital rooms that we stayed in while she was still alive. We spent such quality time together in these hospital and treatment centers that going back and catching up with the great doctors and nurses that helped us along our journey was very therapeutic for me. I took photos of the beds and chairs she once sat in, soaked in the still lingering fragrance of memories shared there, and sipped a cup of coffee to commemorate those moments. I often had to go to places of peace to gather my thoughts. I had a few spots that I frequented around home: the top of the hill at the farm, the lake out past town, and a few other spots where my wife and I shared special memories. One night, I walked to the top of the hill behind the farm and wrote to free my troubled soul.

Journal entry: March 5, 2009

"I sit at the top of the world and watch it go by
It is an endless cycle of sorrowful time-slide
The birds fly overhead; yet again they will fly tomorrow
Clouds continue their watch by day as they endlessly
surface the planet over
The sun still circles, its age-old guard of heat and rays
like a sentinel, lives on to tell the stories
And who am I, just one more story?
Surviving through and past one day, another comes again
A small piece in this vast world of change, and yet
always constant
When I come here, I can feel peace. Nothing here knows
trouble.
All creation sings the free song of liberty in God's
providential care
Careless they continue on, effortlessly living and
breathing in the light rays of his hands
While turmoil strikes my breath away
And pain restricts me like chains of fettered iron
A day gone, another will come
The vicious cycle keeps ticking and turning
Pages of the calendar remind me of the turnover speed
time possesses
And time is gone . . .
Never to be regained
What does it say about a man when accumulated days are
all that mark one's evidence of survival?
Like snowfall, they build on the surface floor of
accomplishments
Lying there as proof, strong, silent evidence, that I have
somehow made it this far
And yet with all my desire I crave for escape
And nothing works. Nothing solves the mystery of
struggle

If only you were here, my love
Wish you were, o sweet angel of escape."

The locusts took from me, from us. What does that feel like? How does one hold such a thing? How can one put into words what it feels like to have the single closest person in life be ripped away from you? God is good, isn't he? Why then, did she have to go? Why would a just and righteous God allow such a tragedy to happen? Why me? Why us?

So many times, when we hit these low points of despair in life, the questions start to arise. We are human. So were the men and women in the Bible. Too often, we think that the heroes of the Bible were elevated onto a platform that made them perfect or superhuman. Too many times, we elevate them to a place that makes us feel as if they weren't made from the same genetic material we are formed with just because their names are printed in Scripture. How silly to think that the men and women of the Bible were bulletproof, exempt from real emotional turmoil. David is a perfect example of how real a man can be emotionally with his Lord. Although we are not completely sure if he was the penmen of this particular passage of Scripture, look at what this heart-stricken man once wrote.

But you have rejected us and disgraced us
and have not gone out with our armies.
You have made us turn back from the foe,
and those who hate us have gotten spoil.
You have made us like sheep for slaughter
and have scattered us among the nations.
You have sold your people for a trifle,

demanding no high price for them.
You have made us the taunt of our neighbors,
the derision and scorn of those around us.
You have made us a byword among the nations,
a laughingstock among the peoples.
All day long my disgrace is before me,
and shame has covered my face
at the sound of the taunter and reviler,
at the sight of the enemy and the avenger.
All this has come upon us,
though we have not forgotten you,
and we have not been false to your covenant.
Our heart has not turned back,
nor have our steps departed from your way;
yet you have broken us in the place of jackals
and covered us with the shadow of death. (Psalm
44:9–19)

Do those sound like holy words to you? Does that sound like something you would hear from a man of God standing solid in his faith, someone filled with God's Spirit? Why do we as modern Christians try to pretend that we are all dignified and okay in situations of affliction and suffering? Do we really feel as if we have to put a show on for the Lord? Doesn't God already know our hearts, minds, and thoughts anyhow? It is silly to even think we need to *try* to look a certain way for the Lord. To be anything else but real, transparent, and raw would be pointless and profitless. God knows us better than we even know ourselves, for he says: "By this we shall know that we are of the truth and reassure our heart before him; for whenever our heart condemns us, God is greater than our heart, and he knows everything" (1 John 3:19–20).

The desperate heart is the heart that reaches the Lord, so why not be real before him? Night after night, my prayers were as real as they get. It was a very confusing time in my life. I asked God many questions. Some prayers, if others only knew, I suppose folks would think I was being fairly disrespectful to the Lord. But isn't God big enough to handle our hard questions?

Journal entry: July 30, 2008

"I lie in bed. I miss her like crazy. The thought that I can no longer be with her crushes me. It is overwhelming. I lie here, looking at pictures of her. She was absolutely wonderful; but no, I can't be with her. It's awful. She seems as if she's still here. It's like she's over at [a friend's house] or somewhere else, and I'm home with the boys for the night. I feel that she'll be back soon, as if she's just away on a trip, and when she gets back, we'll be able to snuggle and kiss and be close in bed again. I'll be able to feel her warmth and soft skin and the smell of her hair. But it's just a false feeling. She will never walk through the door again and yell my name. The only smiles I'll ever get now are in the pictures I so passionately admire.

"This is unbelievable at best. The permanence and concreteness of what happened on July 20, 2008, is still far away. I still don't get it. The thought that I'll never get to see her again, in all my whole life, I just ache. I want to kiss her. I want to hold her hand again. I want to cook her breakfast once more. I want to see her bringing the boys up to the barn. I want to take a walk with her. I want to just look at her and admire her and not even say anything till I have discovered her face all over again . . . and then whisper 'I love you' into her ear before I start to kiss it. All her stuff is still here. She's not coming for it. It's my stuff now. I hope that nobody ever messes it up or moves it. I'd like to leave everything just like she did."

Here is another journal letter I wrote to Becca two weeks after she passed. It explains my feelings well.

Journal entry: August, 2, 2008

"Well Babe,

"It's that time again—the time of day that everybody is asleep in bed but me. And now I lie awake, thinking, dreaming, and imagining you. You were too young to die. There are too many things that we still have to do. I know that you are having a great time in heaven, but when I go do some of those things, could you pop in and join me? I miss you terribly. The realization of the finality of what just happened is enough to make me crumble. I look at your pictures. It's as if you are coming back, as if you're so close, but yet so very, very far away. I want you to be with me again. I want to go on a date with you. Who am I kidding? No amount of new things, gifts, cards you left us, no amount of excitement, distraction, or enjoyment of anything can satisfy me. You are the one that I long for. You are the one that I miss. I married you. Only you.

"I didn't intend for it to happen this way! We have so much more to do, so many more breakfast dates to go on. I have so many more park walks or walks up the road to take with you. I want to watch the lightning crash down all around while we sit on the rocks. I want to paint many new pictures of you. If I woke up tomorrow to eat breakfast on the porch, or at least drink a cup of coffee, would you join me? I so desperately want to feel you, feel your presence, feel that you are still here with me. I want to feel you watching me, feel your company. Even if I can't see you, that's okay. I just want to know you're there.

"I'm getting pictures developed. Do you want to look at them with me? You always loved to look at new pictures. I'd love to have you join me. The company that the boys provide for me as our family is wonderful, but it's nothing like what you provided. Your companionship is simply never going to be closely replicated in any way. You were my best friend, bar none. My companion, my helpmeet, my . . . I can't describe it. You completed me in the most positive ways. You were a perfect match for me. And now I realize I can't see you anymore, which is very, very difficult. I do not want to spend my whole life waiting to see you again. But when I do, it won't be the same. I'd like to be married to you forever. I know the Lord doesn't work things like that, but right now, that's how I feel."

Even though I walked through the land of grief holding my two boys, I eventually walked the journey alone. They both healed much more quickly than I did. I was told that children are resilient and bounce back from tragedy sooner than adults. I definitely found that to be true with my sons. When my boys were bouncing back into action, I was still dragging the past along with me. In their defense, they had a better support system than I did.

They had a dad who strove to be there in their grief, who could understand exactly where they were. Not only did I spend my energy to help them through their grief, but others did as well.

Their young age also helped them out as they could not hold onto their sad memories for as long in their minds. Justin was only three. He didn't really remember much at all except for what we told him from photos and movies and the stories we shared. On the other hand, I seemed to be a taboo subject.

I have found that a great correlating enigma exists regarding the Word of God and people's lives. God's Word is perfectly relevant to your current situation, all the time, no matter what you are facing. No matter where you find yourself in life, in positive or negative situations, a Scripture can always show you that God knows exactly how you feel. David again pens the Word of God, saying: "My heart throbs; my strength fails me, and the light of my eyes—it also has gone from me. My friends and companions stand aloof from my plague, and my nearest kin stand far off" (Psalm 38:10–11).

During grieving, both individuals struggle: the one suffering from loss and the friend by their side who doesn't know what to say or do. Both parties are in an uncomfortable position.

Some people think they can fix your situation quickly and easily, which serves a dual purpose. Think about it and hear me out. If you can fix the problem, not only does the one hurting receive his or her life handed back to them whole and well, but the other party will not feel uncomfortable any longer in that awkward place of confusion. a friend or acquaintance who doesn't understand the true depths of your heartache may simply attempt to address the situation with a trite phrase of encouragement as if it were something you could easily get over. I always despised those clichés. "You will find love again" was one of the most hated phrases I could possibly hear, yet others thought that it would actually be helpful to say those cursed words. Other quotes came with a pat on the back, such as, "This [pain] won't last forever," or "She's in a much better place now." They acted almost as if nothing were wrong and life were just peachy-keen. They spoke words into the wind that were supposed to magically fix everything broken and we could pick right up where life left off before the loss occurred.

Some friends or acquaintances were a bit wiser and understood that there was simply nothing they could say or do to make me feel better. These friends, although they had a greater understanding of the matter, still were unsure how to be or act or conduct themselves around me. Frequently, a friend would come my way or cross paths with me, only to make it blatantly obvious how uncomfortable they were. When that occurred, I immediately felt as if I were a taboo subject.

Looking around the room, I could quickly tell who felt uncomfortable being in my presence. As a result, I adjusted to feeling odd around anyone that I came in contact with. Many social situations soon became awkward. Sadly, I withdrew from other people just to alleviate the uncomfortable moments I didn't want to face. Worse, I felt other people doing the same thing to me.

At first when Becca passed, we were invited to people's homes and parties. Although awkward, at least we had the opportunity to socialize with others. I suppose others have a limit on how much of one's grief they can handle, and soon, we seemed to be forgotten when guest lists were written. Maybe it was easier for other people that way. I can imagine how hard or difficult it would be to hang out and be with someone who is grieving for the long-term. Grief is hard on everyone.

I was quickly treading water backwards in a sense and didn't like the feelings and vibes from either of these two groups of people. Excessive attempts at consolation hurt almost as much as being ignored. Not only did I want to protect myself from this mental torment, but I also wanted to shield my children from the so-called kind intentions and hurtful phrases of other people.

It all boiled down to that I often felt as if I were totally alone, standing bewildered through all this.

This excerpt from my journal describes my situation well.

Journal Entry: Drowned and Forgotten

"On July 20, 2008, the rowboat that carried my life across this great divide of ocean span was found most unfortunate as a wave unperceived crashed and split it wide open. Quickly, as water gushed and flowed, it filled and sank, leaving me to tread. Treading, floating, fighting to keep alive on this mighty journey, I fought with every muscle fiber at expendable reach, all while holding and carrying the only priceless ones remaining. Heavy they were, yet I complained not. To keep alive my treasure was my only remaining reason to stay afloat, and that, I pursued with relentless devotion. Weeks went on. My arms never grew weary. We were out at sea, drifting.

"While wave after mundane wave brought trouble to our survival, my treasures proved life-preserving. Helping, rowing, encouraging, on and on, when the shoreline remained distant, they pushed me to continue. When fog cleared and eyesight opened, these two treasures were the very ones I lived for, and I pressed on with the same strength as if my raft still remained.

"Then, one salty and misty day, an old piece of wood bumped me in the backside. I turned. Without thought or hesitation, I hoisted my treasures afloat, now safely riding this godsend. Only room for two, I was more than happy that they could rest. I gladly watched them as their arms limply lay in peace. I now, however, had to tread the waves alone.

"Weeks went by. Eyesore and weary, my arms and legs struggled to do the simplest of tasks. Treading water was no longer a pleasure, no longer a blessing. My treasures looked at me differently now. The eyes of compassion, sympathy, and grief of this unfortunate shipwreck now turned to resentment that my arms were not fast enough to row us home. Now used as a motor more than a lifeboat, the two encouragements of my survival pressed me in new dimensions, and they forgot how hard it was to swim. Their grief was forgotten. Their arms were refreshed. The longing for rest was over for them. I kept on treading. I kept pressing on. Wave after mundane wave spewed salt and muck over my head, the only body part remaining above water. And the worst was soon approaching.

"The day turned to dusk. The night grew dark. The waves increased in size. The hands of the moon and the forces unseen were making my journey and task much more difficult. To sailors, there are nights at sea when the whole universe is visible in a display of cosmic splendor. This night, however, was overcast with clouds carrying gloom and despair. Dark as the darkest night created, some clouds brought messages of rain; some, wind; some, fear. I closed my eyes so not to see the approaching army of grievous black soldiers. I held the wood my treasures rode. Splinters slowly pushed themselves like hypodermic needles into my skin and penetrated yet went unnoticed until I saw the blood and water mixing. Cold was the water that flowed over me. The Atlantic temperatures chilled my bones. I had no more strength. I released my grip and slowly shifted underwater.

"Much easier was the drift when treading no longer was necessary. I slowly and pleasantly sank farther and farther into a mysterious underwater mystery named grieving. It was peaceful here. I was alone. It was quiet and dark. No longer did I battle the waves. Resistance faded away. I looked around at this mysterious new world. I now could rest. I now could be at ease myself. Or could I? The abyss of emptiness called me.

"After days of absent-minded thoughts, the pain that saltwater burn caused was therapeutic. I bled to prove my heart still beating. The return to my pain seemed magnetic. I lulled myself in pain. Pain became all I knew. There was no life in this ocean current. The pain of the body, cold and dark, and the memory of what was left above was all that remained in this underwater world.

"I remembered my packings. Quickly, I reached for devices of homing. Signals were fired. Callings sent. Excitement like a glowing ember lit up as I watched hope grow inside me. Sure-found friends and family would soon rescue me. The world would see my signs! Oh, how beautiful they were. My smile warmed for the first time since shipwreck and loss. My body no longer felt the cold, for soon I would rest dry and comfortable when they came. And so I waited.

"But they didn't. Save for the trolling fishing net that passed by, no soul was found drifting with me. Once, my hand reached hold of that happenstance net, and hope again gave way to captive thoughts of resuscitation. Oh, how my body pulled hard on the net. My weight filled the tensile-strength limit of the rope's woven fibers. Up I started. My rescue was near! At last someone would carry me to shore, bind my wounds, and salve my eyes. And then, with the same shattering force of a depth charge in the chilling deep distance, the rope fell limp as I realized I had been cut loose. Despair set in instantly as I saw my weight was too heavy for another person to reel in. My grief was too much, and one kind soul thought too heavy to help carry. Thinking they had to rescue the whole, they misunderstood I just needed a tow. And now I was left alone, worse than before.

"My heart sinks deeper than my body, and I watch it hit the floor. I drift into the cold and murk again, only to realize now that no one will come. All have forsaken me. There is no one to help, no one to call on, no one to hold me up, and no one to carry me. I remember those who I would call first. They are all standing on the shore with their eyes focused on my treasures as they float in to bay. They are safe. I can hear the welcoming committee's applause through this watery blanket of muffled darkness. No one remembers me. They know not where I drift. They cannot possibly know my burn, my emptiness, my longings. They are not here. They avoid the thought of searching for me, for the risk of experiencing pain themselves is too great. And so I continue to settle to the bottom. Alone. Forgotten.

"In this place, only my love can help me. Only you, my dear, can hear my thoughts and voice and understand the simplest of my life's details. Nothing escapes the interest you have in me. Even in this underwater maze of confusion, you comfort me in ways others cannot comprehend. In my memories, your gazing eyes are cherished more than the gold and pearls that glisten on the ocean floor. Only you, my dear, can hear my heart. No other living soul can grieve with me. And so, I'm content to stay in this place with you at my side. Once I realize the truth of this dreaded situation named *would-turn-your-back*, it is better, more calming, not to reach for help any longer. I'll just enjoy the drift, hold your hand, and speak soft nothings into your precious ear I long to kiss."

As stated earlier, thoughts and questions plagued my mind. In all honesty, I struggled not to ask God why. As a Christian, we all know that we serve an all-powerful Creator. He is our provider, our healer, and our strength. We know we can come to him with anything, big or small, and that nothing goes unnoticed in his sight. All things must ultimately either be caused by or allowed to happen by our Lord. All things good or bad are sifted through his hands.

With this knowledge, I suspect that all grieving Christians must come to a place in which he or she asks God why he allowed it to happen. It is a natural certainty. We are fallen men and women in a fallen world. We can't help but either ask or demand an answer from God when we cannot see past our own hurts. Hurts naturally blind us. Did I ask why? Of course! I asked the Lord why so many times that I think God probably got tired of hearing it.

I asked him why in the night when I cried myself to sleep. I asked God why when I looked into the eyes of my two sons who now would grow up without their mother. I asked God why when I had so many dreams and future plans with Becca, only to realize that they would no longer be possible. I asked God why when due to her passing, I was left unable to function in many respects. I wanted answers. I needed to vent to God, and I desperately desired that he show me what on earth was happening. Why did he seem so silent when I needed explanations? It seemed as if he had turned his back on me. It seemed as if he was being hypocritical by making all these promises in his Word about healing, only to refuse to heal my wife. It absolutely broke my heart that

God had not answered my prayer. I was as confused as they come. I was a youth pastor who others expected to have all the spiritual questions answered, yet I now had none.

And I couldn't help but be real with my words and prayers to the Lord.

It wasn't supposed to be this way.

Journal entry: November, 2008

"Physical and emotional are two worlds unlinked
Or are they, for the only connection I have of reality
Is a tightly wielded link between pain and sorrow
The physical structure of my body's definition
Is curiously knit, interwoven membranes and nerves with panic and fear
How can this be, Oh love of mine?

"Oh God, I feel so overwhelmed with horror
My view is clouded, shaky at best
Dreams lay, unswept fragments of broken glass
Mirrors they are, reflecting back to me memoirs of
hopelessness, despair, and dreams now impossible
I carry this pain, and none can understand it
Some shine pity, and a somber sense of care
But alone, I stand with my head down, ashamed
I have no strength to trek this journey anymore
For my eyes are weary and sore with sorrow

"Often I wonder why my God stands afar
As if to watch me, and see how I handle this nightmare

I feel your strings attached to me
That is the connection I am aware of
How I am reduced to nothing more!
Oh how have I come this far, that the faith-strong stance
of solid rock I had
Has been chiseled bare to a strand of thread
And this I hang from, dangling,
While my God watches

"Why do I feel your stance so afar?
When will I feel the warmth of your love again, Oh
Creator?
This torture! This overbearing misery!
I have lost hope . . .
Almost

"I want to rage my feelings in destruction
Passionately expressing the inward burn of pain and
anger
My muscles expelling energy of untold power
Draining completely the well of strength I have
remaining
Every ounce of fury spent to the shattering of my
surroundings
And then collapse I will once spent, with tears my only
covering.

"Will then your hand embrace me?
Can the grace of your love surround me in yet that
moment?
Can I feel you again, Oh God?
Will your words have meaning once again, as the days of
old, before the floods engulfed me?
Be patient with my complaints, please

As in fear, I speak them."

If I were to be point-blank honest, I would say that yes, I had a beef with the Lord. My wife and I had trusted him. We were confident that he would heal her. We didn't live life the way the world did; we lived as his Word directed us. We tried to live as examples to all those around us. God was doing such wonderful things in and through us, and we were steadfast and confident, trusting in his deliverance. When that didn't happen the way we hoped, I questioned God and became a bit indignant toward him.

In fact, I had such a beef with God that one day, I drove my old blue Toyota out to the woods where I could be alone to pound on God's chest. I drove to where nobody could see or hear me; I let it all loose. In a furious frenzy of both words and actions, I beat on God's chest until I couldn't swing anymore. I punched my truck, denting it. I let out all the steam as I took hold of God's collar to give him a piece of my mind. I let him know very frankly how I felt and how unfair I thought the whole situation was. Why wasn't he there for me? Why didn't he act and heal? Why didn't he do what his Word was telling me that he would do? Wasn't that what he promised?

It didn't happen.

How does one put a handle on that?

Exhausted, I couldn't swing or pound on him any longer. I slumped into a pile of Jell-O, tired muscles sodden in frustration, and began to cry. The very God that

I had just told off, speaking my mind to and saying what I thought of him, was big enough to hold every punch I threw his way. Like a perfect gentleman, he understood me in my pain. He understood that I needed to get it out, and as odd as this sounds, he didn't seem bothered by any of it. I know this doesn't sound very Christian-like of me, but God stood there, taking it all. And when I could go no more, he simply came down to my level, opened up his arms for me, and let me to sit and cry in his embrace. Nothing was solved in my mind, but God was there to hold me. When I saw I didn't chase him away but that his love, in fact, gathered around me even more closely, I felt as if I had been brought to nothing.

And Job said:
"Let the day perish on which I was born,
and the night that said,
'A man is conceived.'
Let that day be darkness!
May God above not seek it,
nor light shine upon it.
Let gloom and deep darkness claim it.
Let clouds dwell upon it;
let the blackness of the day terrify it.
That night—let thick darkness seize it!
Let it not rejoice among the days of the year;
let it not come into the number of the months.
Behold, let that night be barren;
let no joyful cry enter it.
Let those curse it who curse the day,
who are ready to rouse up Leviathan.
Let the stars of its dawn be dark;
let it hope for light, but have none,
nor see the eyelids of the morning,

because it did not shut the doors of my mother's womb,
nor hide trouble from my eyes.
"Why did I not die at birth,
come out from the womb and expire?" (Job 3:2–11)

Many times, we, as Christians, are expected to dance across each step of life's journey with a bouncing smile painted across our faces. We are expected to handle the hard stuff in life better than everybody else, because we have God with us. For some reason, a Christian is supposed to be exempt from despair and defeat when the world around us crashes down. For me, however, there was no hiding what I felt inside. If given the choice, I would have volunteered to leave this world and join her in heaven. I would have been satisfied. It would have been enough.

Journal entry: Saturday, August 16, 2008 (first Lake Erie Beach trip without her)

"Oh Babe! The sun is setting, and my heart is crushed inside out. This is our moment. It's precious, timeless, beautiful—just like you. These moments, ones like these, the only thing that matters is you. Even though I'm surrounded by people [the youth group], I'm all alone. I feel as if I could walk each step across the crests of each wave and walk until I come to where you are standing and waiting for me."

I remember that day well, forever etched in my mind. Though the support of a church and youth group was standing on the same beach with me, I felt vastly alone, dying inside, pained beyond imagination. The golden wave-top crests reflected in the sun. The beauty of the moment was surreal. I was longing for my wife and longing for a God to hold it all so badly that I would have given it all up just to check out of this life and enter into the next. How I wished I could take the hands of my two boys and walk into the sunset, passing from this life into glory as a family to be reunited again. I would have actually done it if it were possible, at that very moment. I was ready. I was fully prepared. I would have given up this life to be together once more, to all be together again. To leave everything else behind, I would have walked right into the sun. To live in the golden rays of heaven's light, past the horizon into the sunset I gazed into.

What a thought.

What a grief.

Chapter 4
Frenzied Chaos

*I have never yet known the Spirit of God to work where the
Lord's people were divided.*
~ D.L. Moody

*When divisions are rife in religion, it is bound to happen that
what is in men's minds will soon erupt in real conflict. For
while nothing is more effective for joining us together, and
there is nothing which does more to unite our minds, and keep
them peaceful, than agreement in religion, yet if disagreement
has somehow arisen in connection with it, the inevitable result
is that men are quickly stirred up to engage in fighting, and
there is no other field with fiercer disputes.*
~ John Calvin

The sky hangs hazy and heavy, laden with the frenzied
beating wings of ten million strong without mercy. A
military coup, a swarming cloud, a looming, merciless
army of famine, marches on, eager and relentless. They
fly in, bottomless appetites to engulf and destroy; pilots

they are, zeroed in on their targets. Foes armed cruel with the mouthparts of creeping insects, destructive armored agents of death fill the skies surrounding me. A cry for freedom, vain voices raised are drowned out in the relentless advance of the noise of terror, so great and so loud that my ears began to pain. They bleed. A thundering buzz, such a deafening hum, this relentless sonic fright and terror flies overhead, sending a surge of panic throughout the land.

Though the locusts have come and have consumed what they may, I stand amazed; the horizon lies strong with many more advancing. They fly, beating wings of terror, sending confusion into my camp. Should one stand to resist them, like a stream of water rushing around an outcrop of rocky granite, their currents flow around us, their insatiable and relentless pursuits chase away any hint of green tissue yet remaining.

They fly right by my flesh and bone, my cloth-covered skin, with heat-seeking, focused mouths, hungry to engage. Will I survive? There is no stopping this surrounding war. I hold my ears. I close my eyes. I gather those within reach to protect from further damage. I kneel, pleading to God that they pass swiftly. It is hard to breathe as they fly into the current of air I need to survive, polluting it. They beat and brush against my bowed back and knotted hair. A living wind of insects moves over me.

§

"Awake, you drunkards, and weep,
and wail, all you drinkers of wine,
because of the sweet wine,
for it is cut off from your mouth.
For a nation has come up against my land,
powerful and beyond number;
its teeth are lions' teeth,
and it has the fangs of a lioness.
It has laid waste my vine
and splintered my fig tree;
it has stripped off their bark and thrown it down;
their branches are made white" (Joel 1:5–7).

No doubt, the death of my spouse was the hardest thing I had ever faced up to this point in my life. It was agonizing to watch her health decline and extremely gripping to have to say goodbye to her. Regardless of my pleas, my prayers, my begging to God through the night, life ticked on in a continuum without her. Now, only the three of us pirates remained. I held two boys as we were forced to push forward in life. Our opinions on the matter didn't make a bit of difference. We couldn't keep her alive, regardless of our cries. She was now gone forever.

Looking back, some of the hardest moments to handle were some of the simplest things. Falling asleep at night had to be the worst. Nobody liked the time when the house got quiet, when mom's presence was missed the most. We tried to do the best we could to comfort each other and embrace togetherness. We all piled in bed to watch a movie that both made our eyelids heavy and distracted us at the same time. We burned through many a movie to help pass the hardest time of the day. We probably watched that little mouse named Remy make

Ratatouille three hundred times, and the pod race on *Star Wars: Episode I – The Phantom Menace* was another favorite. The boys would fall asleep, and then I could have a moment to decompress.

As we faced the new life ahead, sooner or later, some days slowly became easier. We began to figure out how to live through some of the pain. Of course, some moments were very difficult, especially when something unexpected came our way. Still, life took a different shape as we adapted to getting through the necessities and priorities of daily survival. Clean clothes, hot food, Bible lessons, and moments of family fun were my biggest priorities. I tried to ensure that each day included all of those. As life changed, we changed to meet the demands and, in some regards, were doing rather well. I put Bradley on the school bus in the morning and took Justin to work with me. I only needed to worry about one kiddo back then as Justin could usually accompany me while I was working on our own dairy. The life of a farm kid is an interesting one, especially if you are raised there. Many days, he took his afternoon nap lying in the copilot seat of our tri-axle or tractor as I drove around the farm. Sometimes, he slept on a couch cushion under the milking parlor steps or on the couch in the milking parlor office while I milked the cows.

Routine was my best friend as a parent. We actually developed a pretty solid one, crazy as it was, and life was becoming as stable as could be. Some of the funniest times on the farm were spent trying to be a parent while I worked.

One day, we played hockey in the milking parlor so Justin would have something to do while I managed the cows. His hockey puck took a wild bounce and rolled right down the drain. Oops! There was no reaching it. The next day, the drains in the office had backed up, and water was pooling on the office floor. Sure enough, with the aid of a stiff steel reach, we broke the puck and pulled it out, allowing all the backed-up water to drain away.

Humor seemed to be the best medicine some days. We were now making light of life and making progress as we tried to continue living without a mom to take charge of everything. But little did I know another whopper of a bomb was coming our way. Life never stays still for too long. I could not have anticipated what the next chapter of this wild ride would look like.

My late wife and I had served in the youth department of our church for many years. We had produced abundant fruit alongside some other very important people in our lives. We had established deep relationships with the many youth that came into the program and matured through it. The ministry was flourishing. Great things were happening. A bond was formed in the group that couldn't be found in most other corners of the world. Even guest speakers visiting the program noticed how set apart this particular group was from the norm, a thriving collection of wonderful teenagers, eagerly serving the Lord with us.

Because I had started teaching at a fairly young age, the teenagers in the youth group watched the lives of Becca and I develop through the years as well. They had much to witness and be excited about as the milestones of our lives were shared with the whole gang. The youth group had seen my wife and me as an engaged couple and were excited about our upcoming wedding. Actually, they knew us before we had even begun dating, and some of them even tried to get us together before we went out. They were so amused with their own match-making efforts.

Once we married, the youth group watched us closely and saw us as a godly pattern for how love should be saved and kept. They watched the progression of our developing relationship. They were ecstatic when we announced Becca's pregnancies and introduced our firstborn, Bradley, and then our second son, Justin. They walked through these events with us with joy. God had orchestrated this healthy and viable relationship as we shared a lot of life together with the teens. Looking back now, I can see why so many of them became attached to us. We were modeling the scriptural way of what God-patterned love should look like in a tangible way. The church youth could see real faith and love in action. We were a part of them.

When the day came that we had to announce the news of Becca's cancer to the group, they were shocked; you could have heard a pin drop in the room. The teenagers in the program were very attached to my family, and many of them chose to walk through sickness and death right beside us. Their support was tremendous. Their love was unexplainable. To those of you reading this book who were part of this incredible group of amazing and precious people, our thanks will forever go out to you. Your love and support were absolutely indescribable.

Oddly enough, the same sickness that was meant to quench God's message and ministry in our lives was now being used to amplify it. Our group experienced a tremendous surge of prayer and hope. My wife's heart exploded with care and concern for the teenagers, most notably the females, and she began to minister to them in new and profound ways. As she began to focus on them, she organized and spoke at a teen seminar called "Being Beautiful In Christ." It was highly successful. She taught the teens about many topics, such as modesty, what is really important, and other subjects pertaining to Christlike women. My wife was making lasting impressions on them that would stand the test of time.

Not only were we making impressions in the church, but the outside world was taking note as well. I cannot tell you how many nurses, doctors, and other medical professionals commented to us about what a strong impact we were making. The hospital community was being influenced for the Lord. Our testimony to stay true to our Lord and the love we pledged to each other was rippling through our corner of the planet in mighty big ways. Many people still comment from time to time about what they saw in our relationship and how it impacted them. I am thankful each time I hear a testimony that we made a difference and hope that the values we tried to model are not forgotten.

After Becca's passing, I strongly desired to continue the ministry that God had begun in us. I loved what I did, and our effective and influential ministry to others brought such peace, satisfaction, and purpose to my heart and soul. Little did I know that great and disturbing structural problems in our church would stifle my dreams and limit my effectiveness in this ministry.

Every church body has growing pains, but these can usually be worked out in a healthy way. The church had dealt with small conflicts and disagreements over its lifetime, but none of these set the church so far back as to cause the disintegration of itself. After graduating from high school, I felt led to serve the Lord there and to give back to the church that had raised me. So I began my ministry as a youth leader.

To attend a church and to have a church family are two very different things. Many people around the world just "go to church" each and every week. But to be a part of a church body or family is a different level of connection altogether. A church family will fellowship together as a body. We take care of each other. Not only does the church body take care of itself on a spiritual level, but they also care for each other on a physical and social level as well.

The church visits and prays for people who are sick. They bring a home-cooked meal or two to bless those in need. Those who come up short financially for a month or so can lean on the stability of others who understand their monetary need. People form friendships and meet and cultivate social needs. People are built up, edified, and pointed to the love of Christ.

Growing up, my family and I usually hung out and socialized with friends we had made in church. I met my first wife there. What a blessing it was that two people born and raised in the church would marry and start a family together. I was baptized there. I accepted the Lord as my Savior there.

Unfortunately, sometimes evil creeps into even the body that Christ has bled and died for, his bride, the one he desired to rescue for eternity to abide forever with him. As hard as it is for me to talk about, problems arose in our church that should have never happened. Divisions. Strife. Abuse of leadership power and authority. Politics. Shame. As a change in leadership style and position was ravaging our congregation, so was the destruction.

Two-thirds of the church eventually left, a terribly sad disruption to a quality church of many years. I, unfortunately, did not see eye to eye with the powers that be. No one had any say or rebuttal about what was going on. One by one, those who opposed the new phase and face of leadership were simply pushed out of the way. To make a long story short, I could no longer put my name alongside the new leadership as they made these changes. The flock was being ripped apart, and anyone who stood in the way faced difficult repercussions.

One night, during a meeting, after a horrible confrontation that involved blackmail, I decided to bow out of the church youth program. I simply could not fathom that everything I was working for be destroyed by lies and false pretenses. I could not drag anybody else—especially those I cared for, young teenagers growing up in this terrible situation—through the mud just because I stood in the way of what leaders wanted. I watched what was taking place but could not stop it. So I quietly bowed out.

It devastated the teenagers, resulting in much chaos and disarray in both the youth and the adults. They were angry and confused. I did not agree with the situation or the way it was handled, but I couldn't do anything about it. It is a shame that the church was so horribly disrupted. The church was clearly going in a different direction than me.

Those of you who have never been in ministry may not be able to relate to this chapter. But especially for you readers who are church workers or leaders or who are volunteering your time and effort, issues related to church conflict can be especially difficult. I want to speak in general terms here. God can bring restoration in all things, and I don't want to judge or condemn anyone who was involved. It is my heart and desire that restoration could take place, God's people healed, and leaders forgiven.

My heart broke for the flock caught in the middle of the upheaval and for those who caused it. I will tell you, though, that church splits and betrayals can form scars so incredibly deep in a person that the average church member has no idea what to do next. The church is to be a place of salvation, growth, healing, help, and safety. Instead it had become a bed of thorns that scarred the men, women, and children who had called it their own.

A host of emotions that I almost cannot describe overwhelmed me. All the blood, sweat, and tears of more than twelve years of teaching teenagers went up in smoke in an instant. It was as if a bomb dropped and exploded in our midst, killing and wounding many. I looked around as teenagers and their parents fled in every direction. The problems in the church resulted in a rapid exodus for many of the former members. A broken flock scattered everywhere: to neighboring churches, to home, and even those who sadly quit following God altogether due to the deep betrayal and hurt.

In all honesty, I hope and pray that everybody who was involved has changed and that the Lord has repaired what was broken. One entry shows enough of my heart to tell the story without revealing how bad the betrayal was, so I will share this entry with you. It is a letter that I wrote to my late wife, who was my ministry partner, the one I called my better half.

Journal Entry

"Dear Bec,
"[Someone] tells me not to take it personally, but somehow I cannot. I feel as if I'm letting you down. I feel as if I'm letting myself down. I feel as if it's over.

"I started teaching in 1998, maybe earlier. I have been teaching for a long time. And now I am being told it's ending.

"My heart breaks. I looked around tonight. I know all the stories. I know which kids did what. I know so much about that place.

"I have lasted almost five times longer than the average youth pastor. And now, because of unanswered questions, that's being taken from me. It will change my lifestyle. It may change me.

"I don't really know what to write, since I'm sure, one day, someone will read this. How about this: 'May God be true and every man a liar.' God is always good. Men ruin things.

"My heart is broken because I am the innocent bystander of political agendas.

"You must shed a tear, even in heaven."

That is the only entry that I feel safe enough to share. May God fix the mess and the broken lives the painful church division caused.

And it is an instructive and solemn fact, brought out in the history of more than one revival, that when a whole neighbourhood had been well watered with the showers of grace, no drop of blessing has descended there where a spirit of controversy and strife had obtained a footing— the Spirit of God hovered around but fled from the scene of discord as from a doomed region where his dove-like temper could find no resting-place . . . . Ever remember, that "his work is sown in peace of them that make peace," and no dwelling can be more distasteful, no vessel more unsuitable to him, than a heart which delights itself with matters that provoke contention and strife . . . . Labor with all diligence to keep your own minds in the peace of God, and in your intercourse and connection with others ever to strive for "the things which make for peace.[6]
~ Author unknown

"Stab the body and it heals, but injure the heart and the wound lasts a lifetime." ~ Mineko Iwasaki[7]

Was there pain? Pain hurts the deepest when it is in the very place that safe haven should be. Betrayal? What a painful word! How could I not feel betrayed? I watched a church division split up all the teenagers that I had so faithfully poured my life into. And this at the hand of leaders who supposedly cared for me. Were there scars? The tight connection that the youth group enjoyed was severed right in front of our eyes by something that did not involve them. How could my heart and mind emerge unscathed?

Did I suffer from paranoia? Yes, yes, and a thousand times, yes. When the damage was done and trust was broken—no matter who or what was to blame— a dark henchman of paranoia quickly follows, which declares that other churches cannot be trusted either. This wasn't just my own personal feeling; it was a very popular opinion of many. How can you tithe and support the next church when you just watched the one you served for more than a decade explode?

How can you trust again? How can you regain belief that church is a safe place to worship? Is there such a thing as a safe place for a hurting Christian? How does one pick up the pieces after that and move on? Is it safe to minister or serve again? These questions plagued my mind. What was worse, much worse, was the realization that many souls were betrayed beyond the point of ever entering a church door again. I sadly believe this problem resulted in significant and eternal consequences.

"Divisions in the church always breed atheism in the world." ~ Thomas Manton[8]

It was heartbreaking to see the ministry that I lived and served fall to pieces. We were ushered out: me, my wife, although she had passed away, all that we worked for, and all we served to build there.

The youth group room had a wall with a collection of handprints of those who that had impacted our teens in a special way. Missionaries, graduates of the program, and former leaders were all honored in paint. Becca's handprint was there, too, one of the few left-handed prints. But no more. With the literal painting over of her handprint, so ended our ministry. The kids were appalled. I had no words.

I'm not going to blame anybody. I know that we don't fight flesh and blood. A destructive chasm strike and division in our church only proves further that there is a battle in the heavens. People are not necessarily capable of such destructive behaviors. God's Word even states this clearly. "For we do not wrestle against flesh and blood, but against the rulers, against the authorities, against the cosmic powers over this present darkness, against the spiritual forces of evil in the heavenly places" (Ephesians 6:12).

Was I upset? Yes, terribly. It was a low blow, a strike against me in the most vulnerable of times. I was no longer doing the very thing that I had lived and breathed to do. I *was* an effective youth leader. Did it get any better than that? How can one top the privilege of molding and shaping the next generation, pointing them to Christ? To be dismissed while serving was devastating. On another note, I lost more than a ministry. When I was ushered out of what I felt was my calling and purpose in life, I lost much, much more. The church had been my home. Seriously, this church *was* home. I was now *homeless*.

I had been put through the fire with the decline of my wife's health and with her passing. I was grieving. I was searching for answers that other people search for as well: the whys and hows of life. I was fully convinced that the Lord was going to heal my wife though he didn't. Now my church family was struck with a lightning bolt of division and was devastated by it. My ministry was taken away from me. I no longer had a church home to call my own. I felt aimless, purposeless. Everything seemed to be gone in the blink of an eye, so fast, so insanely fast.

I now felt much like a pirate out on the seas, searching and roaming with no place to call home. I knew that the Lord was still with me. I knew he still wanted to use me. I knew in my heart that even though life wasn't going the way I wished it would or the way I anticipated it would go, I shouldn't give up but should press in deeper. That is exactly what I did. Surely pressing in to the Lord would result in safety and security, right?

Pirates are born to roam.

Chapter 5
The Black Sky

*There are wounds that never show on the body that are deeper
and more hurtful than anything that bleeds.*
~ Laurell K. Hamilton

*Lament like a virgin wearing sackcloth
for the bridegroom of her youth.
The grain offering and the drink offering are cut off
from the house of the Lord.
The priests mourn, the ministers of the Lord.
The fields are destroyed, the ground mourns,
because the grain is destroyed,
the wine dries up, the oil languishes.*
~ Joel 1:8–10

Only a short time later, I found myself enjoying the
blessing of the Lord's guidance once again. Life had
continued, despite the losses I had suffered. Even though
it was slow, healing and growth were both happening
inside me. As the Lord's hand was leading me, I
continued forming bonds with those that were there for

me during those rough years. The boys and I became a little more stable, and we deepened relationships with a particular group of very special people. A lot of positives happened during this time, even though some of it overlapped with the church saga. I had a very special bond with another family from the church that had also unfortunately suffered loss as well. We became very close, leaning on one another for support. We spent a lot of time together and formed a broken but healing new family put together by God's grace.

Before the loss of my first wife, a very special set of children were partly raised in our own home. This family also faced loss: a dad due to cancer. Despite my own prayers and those of hundreds more, a great man of God was lost to sickness.

A mother, now solely responsible for their financial stability, had to continue working to provide for her family. When she worked, especially during the summer when school was out, three beautiful kids would come over and hang out at our house with my family. At first, they just needed a place to be during the day. But our bond developed into something special. The kids became very close to my youngest sister, and they had a blast hanging out on the farm and found themselves on a bunch of crazy adventures. They also enjoyed spending time with my late wife, although she was quite sick. They were an important part of her day. She loved the company, and taught them a lot, especially the oldest.

I sometimes came home to the wonderful smell of salsa cooking on the stove in preparation for canning, a new dessert that kids wanted to try out, or some other creation of beauty that they had worked on that day. Many times some of them would come up to the farm, and I'd hang out with them and see them while I worked. It was a wonderful season, a win-win situation, as they needed a place to be, and we welcomed them with open arms. Their presence brightened our spirits as we could help out their need and bond with them. This wonderful support network inspired love.

When Becca passed, the emotions of not only my immediate family but this bonded family were ransacked. A friend of ours had lost a husband, and now they, in turn, had lost a dear friend, my wife. Not only that, but three children had lost an important figure in their lives for a second time. Despite the difficulty, we hung together, and two broken families tried hard to make the best of the situation.

These three children, who had been somewhat adopted by us, still came over. They had a place to stay and hang out during the day, even though I was at work and Bec was gone. The farm was—and still is—a great place to grow up, as it has countless opportunities for adventure. Our house wasn't a gorgeous model home, but it was filled with growth, development, bonding, and love. In that, the two broken families continued to bless each other. The kids watched and took care of each other and occupied each other during the day. The oldest became a big sister to the boys and a daughter to me as she mothered the two youngest in an incredible way I will appreciate forever.

Life began to sprout and bloom. We found joy in the steps we were taking. We now had others to lean on, and they leaned on us. It was beautiful to share life with other people, and as time went on, love formed as well. We had a place to run to when we needed to share our grief. We had a place of safety to turn to when the church crashed down around us. We stuck together and met each other's needs as we were all suffering due to our losses.

Unexpectedly, a big change began to happen. I formed an incredible bond of friendship with the special person that was in the exact same boat that I was. To my surprise, another woman out there knew just how I felt in grief and loss, and we took great comfort in each other when there was no comfort to be found. It was like finding a raft floating out on the ocean waves, and once I climbed on it, I found a woman there in the same situation. There was a beauty to what was happening. We both had lost a spouse, people who knew each other in friendship at that. She understood me. It was as if my shipwreck had found another soul that I could sail forward with. I began to feel as if life could still be lived and love still enjoyed. What an amazing feeling to possess.

Our friendship progressed into a deeper relationship. Love started blooming. Date nights and day trips to get some fresh air to breathe brought life to our souls. Instead of a calendar of only bad events and memories of past heartaches, we filled it with days of new expectancy and promise. The puzzle pieces fit and orchestrated together, and we thought it was beautiful.

A marriage and a family naturally and organically formed. God seemed to be bringing me (us) back into the promised land of opportunity, and everything seemed great. God had provided an incredible opportunity for us all, as we, a broken family of seven, now were really being molded and formed together.

The two of us wanted hope and blessing in a marriage. Love and life was sweet to the taste. Sunny evening strolls were bliss; moments spent watching wildlife and the world of nature around us were awesome. We spent and enjoyed new adventures together. It looked as if a dream were coming true. I thought that life was coming alive again and that I was receiving a blessing that I wasn't quite worthy of. However, for a man who had already loved and lost, I was very afraid to internally acknowledge this. No doubt, I was falling in love. The question was, should I allow myself that risk? After all, this was a very vulnerable place to be—to find myself in love.

October 7, 2009 (Journal letter to myself)

"You have a choice there, big guy. Let me lay it before you. You have a really big choice. God never said he'd make you drink, but he would lead you beside still waters. It's your choice. It's your call.

"You could let God do the obvious. Go for all the dreams he put before you. Enjoy life. Love again. Be happy. Raise five kids. When they leave, hold and cling, love and chase dreams."

Journal entry: January 23, 2010

"Twenty years from now, you will be more disappointed by the things you didn't do than by the ones you did do. So throw off the bowlines. Sail away from the safe harbor. Catch the trade winds in your sails. Explore. Dream. Discover." ~ H. Jackson Brown[9]

"I'm starting to believe that H. Jackson Brown knew what he was talking about. What would I regret in twenty years? So far, nothing. I always wanted to live my life with no regrets at the end. I say it all the time. No regrets. Twain is right, though. In twenty years, the biggest regrets would be what I was just not brave enough to reach for.

"I think about her all day long. Every time it is quiet. Every time I'm alone. I think of what life would be like if she were with me. I think of her as mine. Am I nuts? I don't want to make the biggest mistake of my life.

"Twenty years from now, I will be . . . how old am I? I will be fifty-two years old. Will I be a happy fifty-two-year-old? Will I have a big family, a family of God's perfect number seven? Will I have a beautiful Chinese woman to make breakfast pears for? Will we still wake up to see the sunrise and have coffee while we pray? Will we have been to the Greek Islands? Will we be a team in God's hands? Will we look at our kids and smile at how we made it through all the trials of life together? Will we still enjoy the simple things in life, like going to Starbucks? Will being together be the happiest part of it all?

"Or will I be too gun shy to reach for the best, and in that fear, face a life of regret to kick myself over?

120

"God has written the most beautiful love story I could have ever imagined. And he topped it off with what has happened lately. God has answered my prayer.

"In healthy ways, I have had the most wonderful, romantic, and intimate thoughts of my brown-eyed beauty. I now see a beauty in her that has been there this whole time. Maybe I just wasn't paying close enough attention. Her eyes are deep magnets, transparent windows to her soul. She is so transparent that she's not afraid to try. I have so many daydreams about her, ever since holding her hand in the car in the J.C. Penny's parking lot. I really could have stayed there all night. I dream of things like cooking together and wiping icing on her face. I dream of holding that hand again. I think about the next time I can touch her again. And when we're old, and all the kids are gone, we will just love each other as deeply and as passionately as possible. Grow old together. Be in love forever, not forgetting that our love is something very few ever find.

"Am I crazy? Who cares if I am! I will be the happiest crazy man ever to receive a present from God. Crazy or not, in twenty years, I'd still have no regrets."

Such beautiful things were forming, such precious memories. We strove to replace pain and hurtful memories from the past with new and exciting plans to look forward to. We took wild adventure trips together and made new memories. We had so much fun making moments of joy and taking time to run and live with fresh breath inside our lungs. We lived life and experienced great restaurants and did the exciting things others would dream of. We were really living.

And so the dream continued.

In August, 2011, we finally enjoyed the bond of marriage once more, and life was blooming brightly. I had someone to talk with, love, and navigate through life with once again. We lived life well, enjoying the accomplishments of dreams and checking off our bucket lists of ideas once only thought of. It seemed as though God had great plans up his sleeve for us. Sure, we had big hurdles to overcome, but didn't everybody? Life was too short to do anything less than live it to the fullest.

During the same time, many people in our former church were lost as to what to do next after the division took place. They had such deep scars and didn't seem to fit anywhere. My sweetie and I teamed up after seeing a void that needed to be filled and formed a make-shift church service to try to feed the sheep that had scattered in all directions. So many people were without a church home or the nourishment of the Word, and we felt led to pick up some of the pieces and provide a Bible study while people were church shopping. We worked well as a team. She was great with details, the logistics, and the needs that had to be met for such an endeavor, and I was more than thrilled to dive into the Word of God and come up with spiritual food for the wandering people to dine on.

The Bible study from the book of Deuteronomy went extremely well. I challenged families to make their homes a place where the Lord's instruction would continue even if they didn't necessarily have a church to go to at the present time. I challenged fathers to lead and mothers to teach and all to keep the spiritual bar high even without a physical building to worship in. I shared that the institution of the family could (and should) be a safe haven even when the church wasn't. They learned that, ultimately, the family was responsible to teach their souls anyhow and that, regardless, we needed to strive to teach and mold our own members while they looked for a new church body. I was very pleased with responses to these meetings. We held services in a public center in our local town. It seemed as though God was achieving purpose in our marriage and family. The spiritual needs of people were being met. Our needs were being met. We were living life.

In time, we started attending a church once again. After bouncing around church shopping for a while, we finally seemed to settle on one particular body. It was very hard to reconnect with another group of believers, as trust and acceptance of leadership were both scarred and abandoned due to our past. Everybody was craving what we had lost in a church, and we could find no duplicate for that in any direction.

It took a long time to finally feel as if we were being fed and nourished in a different church body. It took even longer to feel safe enough to tithe and contribute again. Would we invest our time and energy into another church body, only to be burned and betrayed a second time? In my own heart, I knew I should be more involved. I struggled with it a great deal. But we dealt with so many complicated feelings at hand, which made the thought of going forward too hard. The process took forever.

In time, we hosted a small group Bible study in our home. Members from this new church body came to share the Word of God with us. We really enjoyed leading again. Although we had some setbacks and issues we needed to address as a family, so do other churches and groups. We put on our service hat once again, now useful vessels in life to God's people.

But life grew dark for all of us once more.

§

The last glimpse of sunlight flees as though an enemy dressed with the cloak of early nightfall chases it away. Yet that nightfall hour is not yet to be, and I look for the reason for this sudden darkness. I call to that dashing, fleeting last ray of light. But vanished in an unannounced moment, fled like a thief or a phantom of the night, it is gone in a whisper. The darkness creeps forward, encroaching. The palpable thickness of the ever-black clouds form gnarled spindles of twisted fingers, ugly and crooked hands that reach to grip around all our throats to choke us. The hideous forms of evil swell to blind and cover our eyes, sucking away all strength. They tie our hands behind us. Now prisoners held in black and heavy chains, we all dwell in a pit of despair, a land of ashes resulting from the plague the locusts left behind.

With the steady drip of water falling from miles above, I feel the teardrops from a Father. The death of a dream kills the light inside you. Our light is almost

124

extinguished. Though I strive to keep hope floating, it is replaced with bitter and unwanted pricks, events, shamefully termed as pain and the utter sense of failure. Sweeping through us, we all are affected, each and every one. The vice clamp tightens around us all, closing in on the only windpipe our breath has to travel. Nobody escapes it, none of us, from young to old.

A dark world blankets each one of us, no matter the role or life they play as members of this marriage, this family. Once released, talons retract and leave deep wounds, some voids now slowly filling in with creeping red hints of crimson life; others burst forth with an open floodgate of rich, flowing blood. Can such deep scars ever be refilled with healthy skin? Can such wounds ever be healed? How can one breathe through damaged tubes at half capacity? Life and breath are both damaged and raw. The very touch of air scalds the exposed nerves, a searing pain to the inner core. I look around. We are all hurt and pained, every one. Where do we go from here? It is simply a severing not meant to be.

§

"While he was yet speaking, there came another and said, 'The Chaldeans formed three groups and made a raid on the camels and took them and struck down the servants with the edge of the sword, and I alone have escaped to tell you'"(Job 1:17).

"There are worse things in life than divorce." I read this message from a friend one day, yet I still have to find anything worse. Quite possibly, divorce was the hardest challenge I had ever faced. I saw an unclaimed quote on the internet one day that summed it up well: "Divorce is like death without a burial." It is the one word that carries such a hard-edged, negative stigma with it, such dark connotations, and such a curse of judgment. Those who pass through this crucible, men and women alike, are seen through a different lens or filter, one that is surely there even if people are unwilling to admit using it.

Regardless of the reason or situation for the separation or divorce, a black label of shame is placed on a person, one that is hard and heavy to bear. Divorce hurts everybody: husband, wife, children, even pets. Nobody escapes without some sort of pain and scarring. It is inevitable. I never dreamed that the challenges of recovering from a divorce would be so hard, so real. I can imagine how hard it was on everyone else.

The pain of divorce shows no favoritism as there are no sides to take, no winners or losers. Even in situations that one is justified in leaving a marriage—such as infidelity or other unhealthy behaviors—one cannot and will not escape the pain and damage from doing so. The hurts, wounds, and scars that formed from the very thing that you once hoped would bring joy and blessing, well, it is an extremely difficult pill to swallow—the death of a dream. All parties experience this pain, regardless of the situation or circumstances. Marriage is supposed to be a lifelong land of bliss, right?

Simply put, God did not intend for the unity and oneness of marriage to end, and when this occurs, deep scarring results. The challenges facing the man and woman recovering from divorce are well-known to our society. Unfortunately, divorce is becoming all too common. Without going into detail about my divorce, I just want to use an analogy to describe how divorce looks and feels.

§

Of the remnants left by the storms and the destruction from the swarm of locusts, I look around at the broken pieces left in all of us. The last few scarce and scattered leaves of green tissue and half-chewed blades of broken grass, skeletons remaining of the once-fielded flowers, these, the locusts consumed all we had before taking final flight. Their mouths are never satisfied. They have not left us with anything to hold onto or admire. All is laid waste. What we clung to together has been eaten without thought, concern, or notice. The locusts care not to be kind, and we are left with nothing more than when we began.

All that remains has been chewed to empty lignin fibers, broken structural voids of any nutrition or fill. Only the empty silhouettes of what once was remain. Lives are empty frames without pictures left trampled on the wayside. Shards of broken glass signify the termination of a dream once conceived. We have all lost, we have all hurt, each and every one of us seven, and with this realization, the locusts regroup to move on.

Bare. Empty. The land is void and silent. Where do we go from here? Is there an end to the pain we all feel? I look to the sky, now dark once more with the flight of fleeing locusts. They have consumed it all, and hungry, they take flight to consume another land's lush soul. Their beating wings buzz with anticipation of their next destructive meal to devour. In flight, they block the sun's light of day; I cannot see through the thick darkness. May the cursed beating wings of death in frenzied flight hammer away from my face and eyes. May the surrounding confusion flee far with them. Free me from this chocking cloud of pain. May they flee far from me. May they never return to this place. Hurry on, you unwanted cloud of darkness. Flee and do not return.

§

"Hope deferred makes the heart sick, but a desire fulfilled is a tree of life" (Proverbs 13:12). Of certainty, the death of a dream kills the light inside you.

What to do when the hopes and dreams of a marriage and future together end in shambles and broken pieces of stained glass fragments? Where does one begin to try to pick up the pieces and move on? Divorce cannot truly be explained to someone who has not gone through it. To be separated from someone that you were once united with as one, and to have that relationship severed in two, is a difficult pill to swallow for both parties. The pill sticks in your throat, both a lump of pride and a lump of broken dreams.

I never thought that I would go through a divorce. I cannot speak for my former spouse, but she probably never thought so either. Though nobody goes into a relationship or marriage thinking it could end this way, that's exactly where we were. This was such foreign territory to me. I knew very few people who had gone through divorce. Out in the country in western Pennsylvania, life is much different than the rest of the world. Culture is different. Social scenes are drastically different. We live in a very conservative corner of the globe where you are basically born into farm and church life, you are raised in both, and you are expected to just continue your days in the same. Some people might think that I was living under a rock, but I just didn't know or understand how the rest of the world was used to spinning. Divorce might be common in some neighborhoods, but in my neck of the woods, it was not.

And I felt it.

The days and weeks leading up to the divorce were extremely stressful and taxing. The unknowns of the situation nearly killed me. My fears were large, consuming, and overpowering. Several fears in particular seemed to lock my feet and mind in place as they raised their ugly head to frighten me.

First of all, I feared that my dream would die. In all reality, I did not want a divorce. I did not want my dreams broken or ruined. I really wanted our relationship to work out and our situation fixed. We had been through so much together, and I was desperately trying to hold on to the many positive things in our relationship. Our relationship had started so well, and I didn't want it to end. The fear of the *D* word locked me up many times. I didn't know how to process that fear looming over me. I did not want to welcome another loss.

I was also very afraid that I would lose the relationship that I had formed with my three stepchildren. It was bad enough that it looked as if my marriage were ending, but the fear of losing my stepfamily as well was too hard to bear. The thoughts of losing what I had, regardless of our blended family struggles, plagued my mind on many rough nights. I realized that it was a dark but very possible reality to face. Our oldest had just gotten married, and it was such a joy and privilege to be there for her. I was the proudest stepdad alive as I walked that young woman down the aisle to meet her new husband. I had such a fabulous relationship with her. The other two stepchildren were very loved as well. Nobody wanted that endangered, certainly not me.

Journal entry: July 13, 2015

"I don't know what to say. I am totally and mentally exhausted. Life needs to slow down. I don't like this fast pace. At times, I feel as if I'm gone. I don't understand it. I feel dead inside. Unhappy, inwardly frustrated. I don't know what to do. I am so bummed with everything that I just feel like checking out. I know that doesn't sound very good, but if I'm honest, that's how I feel sometimes. I guess even the Bible heroes said the same thing."

Journal entry: August 12, 2015

"Dear Lord,

"I once had a dream, a really good dream. A priceless and precious love story. A story about how you can take two broken lives and put them together to make a wondrous work of art. I held on to that dream. You gave me a beautiful woman. You blessed me so much. Life was good. My heart was knit to her. My heart was already knit to her kids. I called them my own.

"I dreamed a dream. I knew it was from you. Forgive me, Lord, this dream is failing. It is slipping away. It might be gone already."

Journal entry: November 9, 2015

"Yet I stare out into that horizon like an old salty sailor does best. I am wondering where I will come or where I will go and what this voyage of life will bring me."

I'm not going to get into the particulars of the problems of our marriage. I only want to say that it was now destroying everything, and severe problems were occurring. It was one of the darkest moments of my life, one that I had no clue how to hold, handle, or fix. Maybe someday, I will be talk about the issues, but that day is not today. It seemed like an impossible situation. Years of trying to make it work did not help. A divorce was now the only option I saw.

Although the pain leading up to the divorce riveted me, I didn't feel much comfort after the divorce either. The pain simply morphed or transitioned from one form to another. The initial fears that this, in fact, was happening to me, turned into a newfound shame and discontent that I was now viewed differently from others.

I quickly became aware of how sheepish I felt when I was around people who knew us both. Contact with people who knew us both was extremely awkward. I often avoided these people when I saw them so that I wouldn't have to explain why I was alone or what had happened if they caught wind of the news. I didn't feel I needed to. I didn't think or feel it was anybody's business to judge my situation, no matter what had happened between us. I didn't feel right saying anything about it. I still don't. I would have preferred hiding from the world instead. That was easier. It was very hard to go to public places that we used to visit together. Sadly, that included church, which was possibly the hardest place of all to go.

Journal entry: July 3, 2016

"We went to church for the first time in forever. I have yet to ask the boys about it. It was really awkward. I felt so much shame. Shame to see anybody I knew because they would ask about her. Shame to be sitting among people who might think less of me for being separated or for a possible divorce. Shame that I felt as if I needed to leave and go where no one knew me. So I texted [name omitted]. He said that there's no shame in God's kingdom and that he'd pray for me. [His wife] said that this may be how I feel, but everyone has problems, and I could turn it around to actually help someone else who is going through a hard time too."

In my world, where divorce was far from common, I didn't know exactly what to do. I felt like a pirate again, a nomad without a home. I had no instruction manual to follow now. I felt like even if I did go out in public, it would only expose the black eye I felt I shamefully wore. I didn't want anybody to know about my situation. I didn't want the stigma of the word "divorced" written across my forehead. I didn't want any of it. I just wanted to be left alone to quietly try to regain control of my life. It was an extremely difficult transition because I didn't want to talk about it, I feverishly wrote in my journals, as they were my go-to place or outlet, a vent where I could blow steam.

Journal entry: July 5, 2016

"Last night, I took some of my brokenness to God. He held it. His arms surrounded me and my tears and embraced me with what I laid at his feet. It was wonderful.

"But can I be honest with myself about the brokenness I feel?"

Journal entry: July 27, 2016

"Lord…

"After talking to [my counselor] tonight, I think I have it all wrong. You've been trying to tell me all along. Instead of coping, running, grabbing a fix, escaping, or pretending nothing is wrong, all you are asking of me right now is to cling to you. To press in to you. To lean on you. To find myself in you. You whispered this weekend when you showed me Psalm 21 is all about you and what to do, not the king. You told me again tonight with [my counselor], when he told me to be in you, and everything else will take care of itself.

"'He leads the humble in what is right,
and teaches the humble his way.
All the paths of the Lord are steadfast love and faithfulness,
for those who keep his covenant and his testimonies.
Who is the man who fears the Lord?
Him will he instruct in the way that he should choose.
His soul shall abide in well-being,
and his offspring shall inherit the land' (Psalm 25:9–13).

"All you want right now is for me to get up beside you and stay there. Trusting you. Being one with you. So you can guide me. You aren't going to reveal the master plan to someone who is mad at you or fighting your ways. But you will guide a meek soul who looks to you and waits for guidance. Maybe that's what you want to teach me right now. I get that, and you can lead me further. I had it all wrong. I don't need to worry about the details and unanswered questions. I'm not mature enough for those answers anyhow. But you will keep speaking to me if I just follow you and cling to you, and quite possibly those questions will fade away, and I'll forget this stress.

"Thanks, Lord. I know I need to let go of some things.

"Thanks for being there.

"Love you."

Divorce was not fun. My health was rapidly declining. The stress of the intense situation was slowly sucking the life out of the hollow shell of a body I had become. It was a toxic and daily dose of pain, poison that made me incredibly anxious. Mentally, I was worn out, and emotionally, I had already died. I felt as though I now walked in a wilderness void and free of anything resembling life. I felt as though I were walking alone, and the only one out there to hold my hand was the Lord. The wilderness I now found myself walking through was barren and dry. It was just the Lord and I. There was no vegetation to harvest and collect for myself, I was forced to either cope with starving or rely on the Lord for nourishment. I decided to choose the Lord's hand. It was one of the greatest decisions of my life.

Yes, to be truly honest with myself, it was a difficult and confusing battle to undergo. But the Lord was willing to guide me through this battle. I would not have gotten through it with such grace had he not led my steps. During this time, the Lord took me and taught me very important life lessons even though I was a broken man with shattered dreams. Quite possibly, I learned more here in this barren land than any other place in my life. His Word became alive to me, revealing priceless treasures in Scripture in an extremely enlightening fashion.

I spent lunch breaks at work, sitting with my Bible and diving into what exciting words the Lord had to say next. I also kept a writing log of what God was saying. This place of new solitude ironically allowed my relationship with God to move to a new and higher level. I hope to write a future book on this one subject: how to be led by the Lord. Looking back, I can see that a very difficult but amazing journey began to unfold. What happened in this time period set the platform and stage as building blocks for future lessons and events, many of which I am still reaping today.

I may have been wandering in the desert, but at least I knew that I was wandering for excellent reasons. God was teaching me things I never would have learned otherwise. I had no other way to learn what God had to teach me, save to jump in the desert and stroll around with him for a while. The desert is not a fun place to be, but so many other great men and women of faith and Scripture found themselves there as well in the moments when God taught them the most.

I felt as if I were in good company as with Moses or Paul or even Christ himself, who was found in a similar place with his own heavenly Father. I knew it was necessary to be trained with him there. Although my situation wasn't what I wanted it to be, I was resting in no better place—the Lord's very own hands. That thought brought me consolation and contentment.

It took a while, but I actually began to *enjoy* dwelling in the desert, and it became a one-on-one sanctuary with the King. I was soaking up all the time and attention he was giving me, and my eyes and attention were very focused. In turn, I transitioned from a man with a crushed spirit and no self-esteem to a confident man of God. I suppose I would have gained this confidence no other way, and I became content living in the tent God had pitched for me in this one-of-a-kind wilderness adventure.

Men and women cope with and process the pain of divorce in both similar and different ways. I'm not here to say which one is worse or which sex takes divorce harder, just that there are differences. Men have a different weight on their shoulders than women do. Women have different pressures and stresses in their hearts than men do. Neither one is less important or more critical than the other. I can only speak for myself and for the men out there that carry the same load I bore.

One of the things men tend to carry after divorce is the perceived burden that they were responsible for the failure of the relationship. The marriage might actually have ended for a legitimate reason, but a man will still carry the burden that he couldn't make everything better. Men have been wired to look at a situation objectively, figure out the steps necessary to fix the problem, and carry the weight and responsibility of it. When a situation fails, a man can quickly become disillusioned and think that the failure was entirely his fault. Thoughts might cloud his mind such as, "Why couldn't I keep things together?" Other nagging thoughts might include, "If I were a real man, I could have made this work," or "It must be my fault that I wasn't strong enough to hold us together."

Swiftly behind these types of poisoning thoughts rush in huge boulders of guilt and shame. Men feel responsible for many things that they might actually have no control over. "How will I lead a home now if I couldn't provide the stabilizing glue to fix everything then? Will my efforts work now if they did not work before? Why weren't my prayers sufficient?" The burden often falls on a man's shoulders when the relationship gets rough and falls apart. Due to the innate nature of men to need to be the so-called fixer, they often feel the loss of the relationship as a blow to their own ability to function as a man.

Men also suffer identity issues after divorce. God created Adam in the garden to be incomplete without his helper companion. When Adam found his wife, he was then adequate to fulfill his job and duty for the Lord. Eve completed him. She fit into the jigsaw puzzle piece of Adam and complemented him in all the ways that he was lacking. Their union was meant to be and was perfected as such in a brilliant fashioning of the Lord.

Men today in our culture might put on a face or façade that they don't need a woman to help them do anything, but our very nature was built to need exactly that. A good woman is the finishing touch to a man and the perfect union that the Lord designed them to be. When the union of marriage is severed, an identity crisis can occur inside the man who has been more than his own self for whatever amount of time the marriage lasted.

He feels out of place, dysfunctional. He may have mysterious feelings of social dependence that now no longer exist, causing him to retreat from public events and gatherings. His other half is no longer with him, and he feels the lack of dependency on that party in so many ways. It is kind of hard to explain, but he may have associated himself as "Bob and Marcy" or "Nick and Tina" or "Steve and Shelly" for so long that he isn't quite sure how to remake his identity as a stand-alone creature. The social change is very weird and unexplainable. Many men do not take it well.

Finally, men see themselves as the ones that suffer loss in divorce because, typically, they lose more in terms of relationships with their children. A mother is often closer to children during the childrearing years, and if a divorce occurs during that time, children may become bonded more strongly to one spouse over the other. Men are typically less capable of expressing emotions and feelings, and the severity of this slipping away of relationships can quickly bring a man into a dark place of unexplained depression. Losing touch with children emotionally and losing a leadership role in the house takes a giant stab at his self-esteem and purpose as a man since God wired that into him. When he is no longer serving in that capacity as he once did, the door is wide open for a whole host of negative thoughts and feelings to take place inside him.

I am no expert on psychology. From what I have experienced myself, men may deal with these three sets of issues. I'm sure that women go through a lot of social, mental, and psychological issues as well. I'm just less familiar with their perspective. Regardless of your gender, divorce is a giant, life-altering, and destructive event that will change everything about everybody in the family one way or another. In my situation or yours, the fairytale dream has for some reason soured, and a separation occurred, resulting in unimaginable hardship for all. My fears were many.

Still, God never let go of me. He held my hand in his the entire time. In some sense, a rebirth started to occur. I was reconnecting with the Lord in big ways while also reconnecting with life, friends, my career, and my own identity. A lot of ground needed to be plowed up as the Lord was planting me in a new place and nurturing me in a new way. I watched amazing maturity develop in my life. I went into the wilderness as a broken, lone sailor came out as a tried and tested warrior. My identity was becoming solid once more. The Lord was rebuilding me into something better than I ever had been to date.

Everything is different in the wilderness. If you are currently there, don't grumble or complain in this precious place. I know that this is almost humanly impossible, but the wilderness really has certain benefits. God might teach you the most in this very place.

You might want to look at your situation in another way. In this wilderness wandering, you might develop your personality, character, ethics, values, and your whole foundation needed to walk into the next step of your life. Don't complain in the desert. Try to look for cactus blossoms and appreciate the water when you get a drink. Sweet things are in the wilderness if you allow yourself to see them.

So I lived in the wilderness.

I stood and took the hands of others, and although I suffered a blow I did not expect, I dared to take the next step in life. Surely, life would become easier. Surely, life would level out. How much more could I handle? How much more would my family need to deal with?

Looking into the horizon, surely, it surely couldn't get any worse. Could it?

Chapter 6
The Frames of Leaves Are Broken

While he was yet speaking, there came another and said, 'Your sons and daughters were eating and drinking wine in their oldest brother's house, and behold, a great wind came across the wilderness and struck the four corners of the house, and it fell upon the young people, and they are dead, and I alone have escaped to tell you.'
~ Job 1:18–19

They saw him from afar, and before he came near to them they conspired against him to kill him. They said to one another, "Here comes this dreamer. Come now, let us kill him and throw him into one of the pits. Then we will say that a fierce animal has devoured him, and we will see what will become of his dreams."
But when Reuben heard it, he rescued him out of their hands, saying, "Let us not take his life." And Reuben said to them, "Shed no blood; throw him into this pit here in the wilderness, but do not lay a hand on him"—that he might rescue him out of their hand to restore him to his father.
So when Joseph came to his brothers, they stripped him of his robe, the robe of many colors that he wore. And they took him and threw him into a pit. The pit was empty; there was no

On September 28, 2018, at approximately 3:30 a.m., my life would once more change forever.

It was a typical morning, just like every other morning. It was dark with a slight chill to the air, and yes, I was awake at work, busy on the milking shift—from 12:30 to 5:30 a.m. each and every morning—on our family dairy farm. Our family business had recently lost some employees, and our workforce was thin. A family farm is truly just that—a farm that needs a family to make it happen and keep it running. A family farm demands high energy from all its members. It takes a lot of work. Sometimes it feels as if you are working just to keep the business running instead of the business running for you.

Most people don't know what it takes to run a modern dairy. Modern farm life is filled with many misnomers. Although a modern dairy is very automated with machines to do much of the work, people still need to be there to keep it rolling. Long hours are the norm. That year, we were milking roughly two hundred and fifty cows. In the big picture, that might not seem like many, but for us—my parents, my brother, me, and our kiddos—we had plenty of work.

Each cow needs to be milked twice a day, every day, with no exceptions. Since the cows don't get a day off, rarely does the farmer. That particular morning, I was milking the cows with my mother, and my dad was scraping the barn aisles clean with a skid steer loader and a rubber blade. I left our milking parlor to put a sick cow

144

in a hospital pen by herself and had a gate closed that normally would be open to corral her there myself. Due to the lack of help, I would just do the job myself with the aid of metal gates. My dad was unaware that I was doing this.

I quickly saw and processed what was about to happen. Dad had no idea that I had closed the gate, and he was flying backwards in our skid steer, just like he normally would each day at this time. I knew the gate was going to be pulverized, and we didn't have time or energy to fix anything, let alone get our work done. To prevent the gate from being smashed, I hurried over to open the latch. I figured I would be quick enough. I made my move, quick and simple, but the skid steer backed into it first. With no warning, it hit the metal with a bang. The skid hit and crashed into the middle of the gate with a powerful fulcrum hinge effect. The latch end of the gate flew open with the speed of a strike of lightning. It broke free from the latch and swung so fast that I couldn't even see it move. I actually didn't even know for sure it hit me, because everything transpired more quickly than I could process. The top iron bar smashed directly into my forehead, so hard and so quickly that it bounced off me before I even knew what happened.

Oddly enough, I suffered no initial pain, but for a short second of eternal silence, a deafening ring filled everything I knew. I couldn't hear anything else. The sound carried and resonated at an infinitely higher peal than the silence of the moment surrounding me. It was very much like a Hollywood movie moment, in which all sound is tuned out but the shrilled whistle only the hero of the story hears. To this day, it has not stopped ringing.

Sometimes it seems to be more than I can bear. The gate smashing into my forehead severed a tiny nerve somewhere between my ear and my brain, and I would never hear again out of my left ear. Except for the insanely annoying high-pitched whistle of tinnitus that always remains, only a few frequencies are audible, and those are grossly distorted. That was the first and only thing I noticed. Then came the bright white light.

I woke up on the concrete floor as I was being run over by a skid loader. I knew I was going to get hurt worse, so I tried to scramble out of the way. Scurrying in wet slop and manure, I got to my hands and knees, but the vertigo was already so severe that I couldn't even crawl straight. Like an injured crab, I could only crawl sideways, as my efforts to escape the danger were completely ineffective. Since I couldn't figure out how to move my body forward and get out of the way, the skid loader wheels hit my legs. Fortunately, the floor was wet and messy enough with cow slop and manure that I slid along the concrete instead of being run over and didn't suffer any further injuries to my legs. My dad then noticed me on the ground, and I eventually sat myself up to regain my composure.

I actually thought I was fine. I really did.

I had no initial pain, but in the time it took getting to safety and propping up to take a breather, the pain increased. In all honesty, I thought I would shake it off and get back to work. The body can initially resist pain. As I sat there trying to breathe, the pain gradually increased, becoming so intense that I no longer could open my eyes or even catch my breath. Although my eyes were closed, I could tell that my mom was now frantically rushing over, and I tried to tell them both that I needed to get to a hospital. Moments later, they could see that I would not be able to make the trip without an ambulance.

I only remember parts of what happened after that. Over and over, I have tried to replay this in my mind. I must have passed out between four and six times from when they called for help and when I actually arrived at the hospital. Courageous men and women rushed right into the barn, not minding the wet and sloppy condition I was in from being knocked out on a milk cow barn floor. They needed to put a collar on me and were intensely concentrating. They knew nothing other than the job at hand. From the sound of their voices, I knew that I was in a pretty serious situation. I kept my eyes shut since it hurt too much to open them. I've never been in such excruciating pain, as it was so intense that I couldn't keep from blinking in and out of consciousness. They slid me onto a stretcher, and after lifting me only about ten to twelve inches, the combination of motion and pain was more than I could handle. I immediately threw up. One of the paramedics said that I had just thrown up pure blood. I assumed I was dying.

I honestly thought I was on my way out. When I heard that I threw up pure blood, I figured that my insides must have been damaged too badly to survive. My brother then rushed over and whispered in my ear that he was there for me. He wasn't working that morning but must have run up to the barn at hearing the news of my accident. My mother said she was going to ride along in the ambulance, but I could not see her. There and then, I prayed the most earnest and purest prayer I've ever prayed before. I talked to the Lord, asking him to receive me and my spirit. I was accepting death. At the last moment preceding my final blackout before leaving the barn, the Lord's peace washed over me like nothing I've ever felt before. I wasn't afraid to die.

In that moment, I had a connection with the Lord that was so intimate, so beautiful, so peaceful, that in those ticking minutes, the rest of the world did not exist. I didn't think of or remember anybody else. I had no job or task or certain to-do list that needed completed. I wasn't thinking about what I hadn't finished yet in life nor was I concerned about the people I was leaving behind. It was only me and the Lord, the incredible overwhelming peace that he gave me, and the full expectation of what was actually happening. I was actually being taken to heaven. I couldn't believe that it was really and truly my time to die. I figured I had better give it my full attention.

It dawned on me that you only die once in life and have the chance to be escorted to heaven. So I'd better enjoy it, because it was such a special occasion. I wanted to embrace this experience for all the uniqueness and specialness that it was handing me. I couldn't imagine that it was actually *my* time. I know that sounds odd, but in all honesty, the feeling of connection I had with God in that specific moment was so perfect that I didn't care about anything else. My soul and spirit were ready. They rushed to move me again, and all the lights were going out. My eyes were closed, I had peace, and I fully expected to wake up in heaven.

Very surprised, I caught the bright gleam of a

very large pair of silver scissors out of the corner of my swollen eyes. They must have been pretty sharp, because they seemed to slice right down my body lengthwise, apparently cutting everything off in a single swipe. I realized I was still alive. It was unexpected and odd to me. I wasn't in heaven at all. I was someplace dark and cold. The next thing I knew, I sensed ten or so hands all over my body, working feverishly to clean up the sloppy mess of manure that covered me. They put some sort of shower cap on my head and scrunched it all around to make me more presentable and to take care of the awful odor. I blacked out again from the intolerable pain.

The timetable for all this was most likely much different in reality than it was in my mind. The in and out of consciousness that I experienced, warped, twisted, and bent time into a long drawn out series of memories that made minutes seem like days. A sharp prick pierced the nerve endings under my skin, waking me back up. They were messing with my forehead. A needle pinched me sharply again, and I felt the odd, yet welcome, sensation of the suture passing through the open wounds.

Compared to the incomprehensible pain my brain was wrestling with, I had something else to think about and focus on, for which I was very thankful. No matter how I tried, I couldn't see anything other than the vague blur of a hand and thread. It still hurt too badly to open my swollen eyes. Barely conscious, I was relieved enough to feel someone sewing me back up. Over and over, the thin thread slid through the hole they poked the needle through. I could feel every movement—the prick, the thread passing through, the taut pull. When the last stitch ended, so did my memories. I blacked out again and didn't wake back up until I was in a recovery room. I only know bits and pieces of what actually occurred from those who were there to witness it. My mom later told me that they put me in an induced coma.

Waking up with a skull fractured in two places was not fun. I opened my eyes. The doctor was very blurry, and an exact duplicate of her stood right by her side. I closed my eyes. The vision struck pain deep in my head. I threw up. Each and every time I tried to open my eyes to see what was going on, I became nauseous from the blurry double vision. I immediately threw up again. It felt better not to try to open them. I had nothing more to throw up by this point, and dry heaving up slime was awful. I had to turn my head to the side to avoid making a mess all over my chest and the possibility of choking. Such a simple motion, the mere turning of my head and the motion it involved had unbelievable consequences of dizziness and nausea. No movements were easy.

The next sets of memories are both blurry and incomplete. I again awoke to see peripherally that my mother was in the room. She must have been there for quite a while because she seemed very uncomfortable in the only seat they gave her. People kept coming in and out, asking if I was okay. I know I slept a lot.

A woman was asking me questions, like, "Who is the president?" and "What is seven plus four?" I couldn't answer them correctly. My short-term memory, for all intents and purposes, was completely erased. I couldn't remember anything relevant to the situation I was in or the day and age when I lived. I felt silly, completely confused, and totally baffled as why I couldn't remember things. I searched for words that hid from me. I felt like a vegetable. Why were they asking me all these things? I couldn't remember the answers to their questions, and I felt stupid when the medical staff asked me these things. In addition, their questions increased the pain.

The concussion I suffered was so severe that they called it a traumatic brain injury. The immediate danger was the likelihood of brain swelling, in part due to bleeding in my brain. My sinuses were smashed to a pulp. The blood kept draining into my mouth and throat. I'm unsure to this day if they really knew what was going to happen to me. It was scary. The only thing I was positive of was the amount of pain I was in. Only morphine helped.

I was in the trauma unit for three days.

After further testing, they assumed my brain was not going to leak fluid down my spinal column. That was their biggest fear. I had many CT scans before I finally stabilized.

Upon being discharged, it was almost impossible for me to remember anything, and so I needed someone to come to my house when it was time to take medication, of which I needed about half a dozen prescriptions rotated throughout the day and night. I also couldn't walk or stand. I basically stayed on a recliner all day and all night. I had to pee in a urinal jug, which was embarrassing.

The days and nights ticked by. No position was comfortable. A haze seemed to coat everything, a numbness that allowed me to be in the moment but not a part of it. I struggled to watch television because my attention span was zero, but I kept it on around the clock to keep me company. Not only could I not see the screen, I could not hear it with my new hearing impairment. I watched many movies alone without knowing what anyone was saying. My vision was so blurry that it took a week for my glasses to even work at all and much longer to fix the double vision.

I began several therapy programs. Cognitive, vestibular, and ocular therapy dictated my calendar each week. My eye therapist said that even though I couldn't tell I had double vision, it was there. My brain had shut one eye off in the confusion of trying to make sense of what I saw, and I was told I still had double vision into the fourth and fifth month of recovery.

I could not locate the direction of sounds. I had not known this prior to my injury, but it takes two ears for sound location to accurately occur. When someone knocked on the door or when one of my children said something to me, I looked the wrong way. If the remote fell off the couch arm, I looked on the wrong side of the floor. I am still coping with this and learning, but that was the least of my troubles. I couldn't even stand up or walk, which was a much bigger problem. It took months for me to balance well enough not to use an aid.

Even the slightest bit of noise sent me into crazy confusion. Although I was very lonely and wanted people to come and visit me, I couldn't handle visitors once they arrived. I realized how horrible my condition was as I was happier when company left than when they were with me. It was just too hard on me, a catch-22. I hated to be lonely, but I couldn't handle company. This slowly chipped away at me socially and psychologically, and relationships—even very important ones—began to suffer as I simply couldn't be around people for any real length of time. It was even hard to have my kids in the same room with me if they were quiet. What a burden I faced. I felt terrible. To love people but not be able to physically handle their presence was mentally debilitating to me. Many times, I felt the emotional and psychological battle was worse than the physical pain.

The confusion that I faced was another daily battle. Compounded by my severe memory impairment, I found myself lost frequently. Whenever I walked to another room with my cane, I forgot why I went there. People told me things, and I could only remember what they said long enough to turn around and walk the other way.

One day, against doctor's orders, I was taking a shower. I wasn't supposed to shower for fear of falling over due to almost zero balance. I felt disgusting, very grimy and gross, so I took one anyhow. Even though the water was hitting me in the back and I was naked and wet, I forgot where I was and what I was doing. For the longest moment, I tried to remember why I was there. I had to talk to myself. "Why am I here?" I pondered hard and thought deeply. It sounds silly, but that's how far my mind was gone, and it took a long while for me to put two and two together to realize that I was in the shower to wash myself.

The medications were also altering my thoughts,

and one day I thought I saw a cute fuzzy rat sitting on the floor beside me while I was watching television. I was so relieved, because I needed one anyway to feed to my boa constrictor, and I couldn't drive to the store myself to buy one. Now that's far out.

Now that I brought up my boas are brought, they were actually calming friends. Day after day, I watched Carla and Clarissa move slowly and slither around their terrariums. They never made any noise. I could talk to them without any hectic chaos or confusion. I could still care for them since they were completely self-sufficient anyhow. During the night, when I would wake up in pain, they were right there to greet me. On the nights I couldn't fall asleep, they were also there to keep me company. They didn't tire of spending silent time with me. I didn't need to entertain them as I did other company. I could handle their quiet and stable companionship. They became important to me and to my recovery, as much as eight-foot snakes could be.

Little by little, the expectation of jumping right back in the mix of things and getting back to work turned into the disappointment that I would be handicapped much longer than I expected. Prior to my accident, I was very active and enthusiastic about spending time with my boys and doing my best at work. We often went on great adventures together as a family. We went bouldering in the Laurel Mountains, hunting and fishing together, on camping trips to awesome places, and even took a kayaking trip in the islands of Maine. We lived like pirates, seeking adventure wherever the wind blew us, and pushed the limits of what three guys could do to have fun.

But now all that fun came to a screeching halt. I spent my days all the same—just trying to make it through the next twenty-four hours as the tremendous pain wore on me. Those of you suffering from chronic pain can testify to this, as it starts to break you down after a while. You become a bit snappy with people. It turns you into someone who you normally are not. I suffered from migraines that lasted for days. I had four- and five-day-long headaches that were invincible to any pills. I could not get rid of them. I just had to close my eyes and ride them out. This terrible condition lasted a very long time.

I became very disappointed, disillusioned, and depressed. I began grieving my health. I know that a Christian man should stay strong through trials, but I had been handed so many hard times in the last few years that I wasn't sure how much more I could take. Difficulties were really stacking up in my life at this point. In addition to the losses in my past, I was now grieving my health—a whole different ball game. Though I tried to be intentionally strong, I couldn't help but watch depression set in, as I was bound to a chair for weeks and months on end.

I mourned the loss of my hearing. The grim realization formed inside that it wasn't coming back. It was a hard lump to swallow. I had to walk with a cane everywhere I went, and I forgot everything I was told. The inability to socialize was killing me. On top of all this, the pain made life almost too hard to bear. I watched relationships suffer that ordinarily would flourish. It was as if my hands were tied as I was forced to sit and

155

helplessly watch life deteriorate all around me.

My boys were handling the situation well, but as time passed, they began to grieve the loss of dad's health too. Tensions started brewing in our home. My once treasured man-cave became a place of silence. Everybody had to be quiet for dad all day, every day, a very difficult request to ask of two super active teenagers. I felt horrible about it, but I was stuck and could do nothing about it. The only social activity we could do to bond with each other was to watch Netflix or stream movies, which they eventually grew tired of as well.

"Anything that's human is mentionable, and anything that is mentionable can be more manageable. When we can talk about our feelings, they become less overwhelming, less upsetting, and less scary.
The people we trust with that important talk can help us know that we are not alone." ~ Fred Rogers[10]

In an attempt to regain a footing in this new world of chaos, I turned to some of my mentors. I wrote to them, explaining my injury and my situation. I tried to gain a real understanding of where I actually was in all this. I asked them for prayer. I turned to loved ones to pray for my pain. I was encouraged to pray by some. Although I was trying my best, I was no doubt turning inward and closing up.

Depression stood at the door.

"Then Judah said to his brothers, "What profit is it if we kill our brother and conceal his blood? Come, let us sell him to the Ishmaelites, and let not our hand be upon him, for he is our brother, our own flesh." And his brothers listened to him. Then Midianite traders passed by. And they drew Joseph up and lifted him out of the pit, and sold him to the Ishmaelites for twenty shekels of silver. They took Joseph to Egypt" (Genesis 37:26–28).

Not only did depression stand at my door, it was asking permission to consume me. "Then Job arose and tore his robe and shaved his head and fell on the ground and worshiped. And he said, 'Naked I came from my mother's womb, and naked shall I return. The Lord gave, and the Lord has taken away; blessed be the name of the Lord.' In all this Job did not sin or charge God with wrong" (Job 1:20–22).

Chapter 7
All Laid Bare and Wasted

And so rock bottom became the solid foundation on which I rebuilt my life.
~ J.K. Rowling

Then Satan answered the Lord and said, "Skin for skin! All that a man has he will give for his life. But stretch out your hand and touch his bone and his flesh, and he will curse you to your face." And the Lord said to Satan, "Behold, he is in your hand; only spare his life."

So Satan went out from the presence of the Lord and struck Job with loathsome sores from the sole of his foot to the crown of his head. And he took a piece of broken pottery with which to scrape himself while he sat in the ashes.
~ Job 2:4–8

Depression knocked at the door, begging me to answer.

"As soon as his master heard the words that his wife spoke to him, "This is the way your servant treated me," his anger was kindled. And Joseph's master took him and put him into the prison, the place where the king's prisoners were confined, and he was there in prison" (Genesis 39:19–20).

Depression is a prison, a deep pit with no water. Once thrown in, there is no refreshing of the soul to be found. Joseph was sent there, and I felt as if I were in that exact same spot as well.

When the light flicker of life leaves the eyes of the wounded, the ability to continue moving forward is almost impossibly overwhelming. Depression does just that. It takes the small amount of life left remaining and drains it out of you through unnoticed leaks and pores. Other people cannot understand it and are often critical of it. They can't see it through the perspective and eyesight of the one suffering from it. They just don't get it.

Unless you have wrestled with this firsthand, you cannot fully comprehend or understand depression, this mysterious beast, on your own. In my own personal struggle, people told me, "Just be happy!" But telling a person suffering with depression to be happy is almost as ludicrous as telling someone with a broken arm to start lifting dumb bells. It simply cannot be done. Too many components need to be taken care of and addressed first.

"Mental pain is less dramatic than physical pain, but it is more common and also more hard to bear. The frequent attempt to conceal mental pain increases the burden: it is easier to say 'My tooth is aching' than to say 'My heart is broken.' ~ C.S. Lewis, *The Problem of Pain*[11]

In the world we live in today, depression is quite

common. I won't go into the topic of clinical depression, how many people truly are depressed, or what clinical depression is from a medical standpoint. What I do know is what depression feels like, and it is not pretty or enjoyable.

Regardless of one's opinion, scientific explanation, or viewpoint on this hot topic, real people really do experience depression. It is an extremely difficult enemy to fight, mainly due to its invisibility. It doesn't show up on an x-ray or an ultrasound. Depression does not follow all the normal laws of science. Quite a bit of mystery surrounds it, and treating it also comes with varied opinions and complications and is often based on trial and error. People go through it on different levels, intensities, or scales. Some people fight it harder than others, or for longer durations of time, but most people can remember at least one moment in their lives when they felt seriously depressed. Chemical, hormonal, or physical triggers can lead to depression. The specific explanation for it doesn't really matter. I felt it. It was deep. It was dark. It wasn't fun.

"What the cutting locust left,
the swarming locust has eaten.
What the swarming locust left,
the hopping locust has eaten,
and what the hopping locust left,
the destroying locust has eaten" (Joel 1:4).

It's difficult to explain depression to someone who isn't depressed. When you suffer from depression, you look and feel silly, sometimes even stupid. You are embarrassed. Shame is painted all over your face and body. Due to these negative, self-destructive feelings, you retreat. You often feel a total lack of energy with no drive and no gumption. What you are passionate about and previously enjoyed becomes stale to your taste. You even lose the desire to pursue what you like best about life. Activities and relationships lose their meaning. Many people experience weight gains or losses and feelings of hopelessness or abandonment. Your thoughts can spiral out of control, often getting the best of you and putting you further into a deep hole of gloom.

It feels as if there's no way out.

§

The swarms move on. Nothing is left; nothing remains. I look around. The bare carcasses of hollowed trees match the frail, thin-framed skeletons of what once were mighty stalks of grass, former soldiers of golden flowing grain and meadowlands. They are laid waste now, and a somber song fills the air. The locusts have taken flight and moved on after consuming everything previously green. The totality, the finality of life in the field is no more. Does life still remain? Has anything survived this plague of darkness? Is there not a single stem remaining that might yet produce? Open, barren plains speak only sadness in a melancholy chant of woe. The storm has come and gone, the locusts have had their full, and only I am left to mourn it.

The pain and sorrow is more than I can bear, for my life has been lived in futility and deep oppression.

The waves wear and erode at my strength. They have crashed harder and harder against me the longer I live. I have suffered many blows in years past, but this one is terrible, all-consuming. This may be the final and ultimate strike. How can I recover from such a scene as this? Life has been carried and swept away from my eyes. The stormy gale blows hard, thrashing against me. No flicker of candlelight remains, and I have no strength or care to try any longer. What will keep my feeble legs moving forward? Not the drive or desire inside me, for it is diminished beyond the amount necessary to take even the next step. Who can come to my side? Who would bear this burden with me? Can anything dull the pain I feel inside?

Day by day, time ticks by in an ever-marching continuum of pain. I have lost a wife and now a second. A family is divided, and my soul is searching for answers. Everything I once had has been stripped from my hands: my soul mate and my ministry. The church I attended is now a broken mess, and the family I called my own is divided. Is there any place to stand in security? Now, even my health is gone, as I lie here resting, resting from the ever-present, resonating noise in my ear, resting from the ongoing pain in my head each and every day. I can stand against the foe of physical pain if I desire, but mental, psychological, and emotional pain is now beyond my limits. When will it end? When will I see the light again?

I search and reach for something to dull the pain. Something must work. Something must be of aid and rescue. The waves and rough seas have now calmed. The once stormy sea has lulled in the drifting doldrums, a sea without the wind to blow me any farther. In this place, I feel tremendously alone. I drift as if on my very own raft, barely afloat, with no soul in sight to bid me good day. Day after day, I drift, asking the same questions, only to circle back around to the same conclusions. I am alone in this house, though others live with me. The presence of this enemy of solitude changes the way I see everything. I drift lonely. Endlessly.

Yet there on the horizon, through water flat and calm, the swirling sense of another disturbs the glassy liquid mirror my eyes enjoy.

And the mermaids come.

In the distance, they approach swiftly, barely covered by the swirling of dark top waters. Those swirls, eddies of deep black murky water cloaking their arrival, evidences that they abide under me, hiding, until they are unveiled right before me. They come so subtly, disguised as angels of light, yet feasting on the souls of men. They have found me in my despair, singing promises of well-kept feasts and homes of health and substance. I gaze at the beauty they bring in their faces full with assurance. One kisses me. But yet as the taste is still on my lips, a shallow core opens, revealing their deceit.

They cannot produce the reality they pledge. The promise of escape is vain. The contract of stability these evil beings propose holds no truth, stability. Yet many a sailor drifting about has let their eyes be seduced by them, and many have been taken down, tangled in the depths of the deep. All because of the hint of promise twinkling in their pretty eyes, that gleam of hope, that by their kiss the pain may cease. Shall I, too, fall to the ways and shortcuts of life, with mere Band-Aids of coping in an attempt to free myself of this torture? Shall I stoop to unhealthy methods and means to survive the pain and toil? Or I shall wipe the taste of that kiss off my lips, for vain is the help of the mermaids that encompass me.

Depression returns once again.

§

Depression is a terrible weight to bear.

When everything is going wrong and one blow after another beats against us, we can easily fall into the pit of depression. To the depressed person, life seems like a deep black hole. In my opinion, the easiest way to explain depression to someone on the outside of it is to use the analogy of this cosmic mystery. In a black hole, some gravitational pulls are so strong inside the event horizon that not even light can escape. It is impossible to see inside this mystery because no light can escape, entering the viewer's retinas. If light waves can't enter our eyes, we see nothing. In the same way, no outsider can truly see into the depression of another. The light simply doesn't reflect back to us to allow outsiders to understand inside it.

Once we are sucked into the black hole of depression, it is almost impossible to escape. No visible light can shine out for other people to accurately see what we are dealing with inside. Others cannot possibly understand or fully sympathize with it as it is so complex. The unknowns of what lies inside that place are inconceivable. Others aren't actually in it, and so they cannot see where or how you are positioned inside. The gravitational pull is so strong around a black hole that time and space are distorted, making its surroundings very difficult to observe.

In the same way, the soul suffering from depression has a skewed and off-kilter perspective. Observations are twisted, and truth is deformed and misunderstood. The hole of depression bends and warps all perceived reality, changing the very nature of everything on the outside. There, even genuine help may be perceived as a threat. A close loved one may be perceived as judgmental or critical. Even the closest friend may not truly be able to help you. Depression is a beast of its own nature and extremely challenging to fight. It is very difficult to climb out of its hole.

One of the most problematic aspects of depression is the catch-22 of its nature. When you feel depressed, you tend to retreat into a corner to hide and feel better. You feel safer when you don't have to let anyone else in. Secrets don't betray you there. The high walls shield you from any more hurt or pain. The problem with that kind of philosophy is that no one else is there with you. You are isolated. Too quickly, you realize this. You stand there, alone, all by yourself, and in that, you become terribly lonely. Because of the intensity of the loneliness and despair, you don't have the necessary strength to escape the black hole. This, in turn, only makes you feel worse about yourself, and you retreat further.

With the deeper state of reclusiveness, the vicious cycle continues, an unavoidable loop of pain. You don't feel like being around the people who can help you. You don't want them to see you this way. You are self-conscious as you don't want others to see you sad or crying. You don't want to be fake, and you don't want others to see your real feelings of disappointment and despair. The fears inside you and the distorted perceptions worsen your situation, preventing you from helping yourself. Nothing helps.

As such, people sometimes run to unhealthy forms of coping, such as the metaphor of the mermaids. If you're not careful, the mermaids will take you to a dark place of no return. Even though they promise a temporary relief, their lies are hollow and shallow. Going back to the analogy of the fields stripped bare by the locust's destruction, it is like the promising sight of beautiful refreshing rainclouds that instead bring only dry strikes of lightning that burn the wasteland to ashes. Many people let life become ashes before they ever seek help.

"No evil dooms us hopelessly except the evil we love, and desire to continue in, and make no effort to escape from." ~ George Eliot, *Daniel Deronda*[12]

It is hard to find real help. The walls the depressed person has built around them, combined with the disillusionment of his or her perception, makes it difficult for the person to crawl out of the hole on their own. They commonly hit rock bottom before they take any real steps of advance.

Should you be ashamed if you feel depressed?

Excuse my bluntness, but if you believe that people should always be hearty and chipper, please read your Bible again. Depression is a real issue that comes against real people, and many of those people are the heroes and heroines of Scripture. Think about it for a minute. David often became depressed throughout his life during times of great stress and pressure. Here are just a few examples.

"Be gracious to me, O Lord, for I am in distress;
my eye is wasted from grief;
my soul and my body also.
For my life is spent with sorrow,
and my years with sighing;
my strength fails because of my iniquity,
and my bones waste away.
Because of all my adversaries I have become a reproach,
especially to my neighbors,
and an object of dread to my acquaintances;
those who see me in the street flee from me.
I have been forgotten like one who is dead;
I have become like a broken vessel" (Psalm 31:9–12).

"Save me, O God!
For the waters have come up to my neck.
I sink in deep mire,
where there is no foothold;
I have come into deep waters,
and the flood sweeps over me.
I am weary with my crying out;
my throat is parched.
My eyes grow dim
with waiting for my God" (Psalm 69:1–3).

"Deliver me

from sinking in the mire;
let me be delivered from my enemies
and from the deep waters.
Let not the flood sweep over me,
or the deep swallow me up,
or the pit close its mouth over me" (Psalm 69:14–15).

Do those sound like holy words from a Christian man or woman of God? Does that sound like something one would find in Scripture? Yet how many times in the Bible do the patriarchs of faith and hope say that they are downcast or depressed? Some are even at their wit's end and ready for their life to be over. The Bible is a real collection with stories of real people. Period. God put his words together for a real reason. Yet even in this blessed book, we see depression in the people held before us as models to us all. They were really, truly real. No human is above being human. We can face the laws of reality or the terms of agreement. We are all created a little lower than the angels, with real feelings, emotions, and psychological issues. Let me illustrate this point with clarity as we walk through just a few passages of God's Word.

You might be shocked to read that Moses, the great leader of the new nation marching out of Egypt, was so weary he asked God to kill him.

Moses said to the Lord, "Why have you dealt ill with your servant? And why have I not found favor in your sight, that you lay the burden of all this people on me? Did I conceive all this people? Did I give them birth, that you should say to me, Carry them in your bosom, as a nurse carries a nursing child,' to the land that you swore to give their fathers? Where am I to get meat to give to all this people? For they weep before me and say, 'Give us meat, that we may eat.' I am not able to carry all this people alone; the burden is too heavy for me. If you will treat me like this, kill me at once, if I find favor in your sight, that I may not see my wretchedness." (Numbers 11:13–15)

Elijah, the crazy-bold prophet of God who had so much faith he poured water on his sacrifice and stood up to the prophets of Baal, later became depressed to the point of death. "But he himself went a day's journey into the wilderness and came and sat down under a broom tree. And he asked that he might die, saying, 'It is enough; now, O Lord, take away my life, for I am no better than my fathers'" (1 Kings 19:4).

Jonah, who should have had such joy and relief at a second chance on life and his purpose in the Lord, ended up thinking that death would be better than the life he was living. "But it displeased Jonah exceedingly, and he was angry. And he prayed to the Lord and said, 'O Lord, is not this what I said when I was yet in my country? That is why I made haste to flee to Tarshish; for I knew that you are a gracious God and merciful, slow to anger and abounding in steadfast love, and relenting from disaster. Therefore now, O Lord, please take my life from me, for it is better for me to die than to live'" (Jonah 4:1–3).

Jeremiah the prophet, who would write such deep words of Scripture, was depressed beyond measure. He was so deep in despair that he loathed his own day of birth.

> Cursed be the day
> on which I was born!
> The day when my mother bore me,
> let it not be blessed!
> Cursed be the man who brought the news to my
> father,
> "A son is born to you,"
> making him very glad.
> Let that man be like the cities
> that the Lord overthrew without pity;
> let him hear a cry in the morning
> and an alarm at noon,
> because he did not kill me in the womb;
> so my mother would have been my grave,
> and her womb forever great.
> Why did I come out from the womb
> to see toil and sorrow,
> and spend my days in shame? (Jeremiah 20:14–
> 18)

If those men of the Bible are not good enough examples of the struggle with depression, then maybe we should look at our Savior himself. Jesus, the Son of God and the Lord of glory, was fully God while still fully human. He experienced life in every real way, just like you and I. Though we usually don't picture Christ as an emotional person, the real Jesus of the Bible was often upset, sad, disappointed, angry, grieved, and sorrowful. This is not the Jesus we tend to remember, but how could he be fully human without experiencing all these human emotions? Even in prophecy, Isaiah describes him in this way: "He was despised and rejected by men, a man of sorrows, and acquainted with grief; and as one from whom men hide their faces he was despised, and we esteemed him not. Surely he has borne our griefs and carried our sorrows; yet we esteemed him stricken, smitten by God, and afflicted" (Isaiah 53:3–4).

Is it wrong or sinful to feel depression when it comes? Should we feel ashamed that it is a real struggle for us sometimes? Should we be afraid to admit it, try to conceal it, or even attempt to hide it from God and others? Well, let me ask you, were these emotions wrong for David, Moses, Jeremiah, Job, or even Christ himself? Why in the world do we try to act as if we as Christians should never be depressed? We live in a real world where real problems happen to real people with real emotions. We can become trapped in them. We have nothing to be ashamed of or embarrassed about if we suffer from depression. As Christians, we need to understand that if Jesus was described as a man of sorrows, then I shouldn't put much pressure on a struggling brother or sister who is down in the dumps about their current situation. Give the hurting soul a break and don't make their situation worse. People can't just become instantly happy. It takes work, very intentional effort, and a lot of prayer on the part of many around the afflicted person.

When we truly love and want to help a person battling depression, we really need to meet them *in* their pain and *identify* with them. In time, this will give us an in to help the person out. Although we don't want them to stay that place, sometimes we must roll up our sleeves and get into the trenches with another to truly start the healing process.

Yes, in my situation, I became terribly depressed. As if it weren't enough that the last fifteen years had beaten me to a bloody pulp, I did not do myself any favors by moving back into my old home after my divorce. Although I really wanted to be back home where I could feel secure, it didn't turn out exactly as I expected. It was very bittersweet.

On one hand, I welcomed the refreshing feeling of being back home. Three pirates tried to live life to the fullest. We lived life well and enjoyed being swept whichever way the wind blew us. We went on all sorts of new adventures as we regrouped and bonded. We made our pirate cove into a bachelor's crash pad of sorts. When people came over to visit, as soon as they walked in the door, their faces showed what they were thinking. Almost instantly, guys were wide-eyed and amazed, almost jealous of the environment that we had created. But women tightened up and acted as if they had just walked into a dark alley with no street lights, instinctively becoming a bit leery.

We hung up all sorts of guy stuff all over the house to make it cool, as that was all the decorating we knew how to do. Kayak paddles hung above our windows, a Jolly Roger was on the wall, our whitetail deer trophies and antlers graced our game room, and we displayed our guns and hunting rifles in a nice gun cabinet. We didn't stop there. All the curtains came down as we were convinced that men didn't have curtains.

One winter, we even set up a work station on the dining room table and tore apart my son's 250cc four-stroke racing engine to rebuild it. The totally cool house oozed manhood and testosterone. At one point, we shared the house with two eight-foot-long Colombian red tail boa constrictors and two ball pythons. Friends loved coming over to hang out, sleep over, and live the dream of a PlayStation world or of riding quads or dirt bikes around the farm. People enjoyed watching the snakes eat their next meal. We even had a trolling motor leaning in a corner, though I'm not sure why. We didn't just have a man cave; it was a whole man house.

But I didn't fully anticipate the second story we had to tell. When we moved back home, we walked into a house filled with memories, memories that we hadn't visited for a very long time. Every room had a sense and scent of the way Mom had left it. Each corner stored a memory that I had not thought of until seeing the house again for the first time in years. The flood of emotions and reminders of sweet moments came rushing in.

The night that my late wife and I videotaped a movie for our first son to watch after he was born sometime in the future, telling him how excited we were waiting for him, played in my mind. The swing that we built for our children was still outside. The hallway that Justin used to push his walker around while Mom was watching him looked exactly the same. All these things and thousands more were brought to mind. Becca and I had shared so many sweet moments there together, ones expressing our love for one another and the start of a family as evidence of that love.

After these came the painful moments. The chair that she sat in for so many hours while sick with cancer was still there too. The sunlight came in the same way through the back door as when it did the day the whole church came over to pray for her. The front porch still remained, just as it did when her hair was short as she was recovering from chemotherapy. She sat there, sipping tea, wrapped in a robe to keep warm.

All those memories plus many more rushed into my mind, and I wasn't sure how to hold, handle, or process them. Day after day, whatever we did had another memory attached to it. We had no relief from them. I guess I was glad for those memories, but it was incredibly painful to have them stare me in the face all over again. What I didn't realize would happen was, in fact, happening. I was grieving a second time.

After my accident, life became incredibly more difficult. I was already grieving all the former losses I've mentioned. In addition, I felt horrible despair at grieving the loss of my health. The accident that bound me to a chair gave me too much time and space to think. I had no escape from the silence, no escape from the four walls that entrapped me in depression. I was depressed because Becca had died all over again to me. I was depressed because I had lost the hopes and dreams of promise that a second marriage could bring, a second marriage that ended in pain, scars, failure, and divorce. I genuinely missed some things about her too.

I was depressed that I was all alone, single, and sentenced to this prison cell called a living room. I couldn't handle company, but I couldn't handle solitude either. I felt incredibly, utterly, and desperately lonely— the loneliest I have ever felt in all my life. With that loneliness came a depression unlike any I have ever known before—a deep, dark hole that I simply fell into, unable to resist its pull. It seemed futile to fight the gravitational tug. The loneliness was a force to be reckoned with, an irresistible foe to succumb to, the darkest place I have ever been. I never want to return.

Journal entry: October 19, 2018

"Today was a most confusing day of challenges, a day I'm not sure how to hold or handle. A day lost in thought yet spinning still. Rehab, which is supposed to help, is torture and stretches me to the limits of what my body wishes to endure, all while my mind is asked to collect and contain the remnants.

"I am far too exhausted to handle what lies in my hands, on my heart.

"I couldn't stay in the walled confines of memory and heartache. Outside, I find only additional pictures, forgotten but owned. The rustle of the corn leaves. The late autumn sky. Golden lancets of love cast to earth by the sun, only fleeting, fading in strength. The roll of autumn winds carry your song to such a heavy heart. I cannot run from you today. I would not wish to either, my dear. It swallows me, perhaps as the nightmares that chase away my sleep at night. It wraps around my head as only a shadow of reality seen by my weary eyes. I am crying. Yet no moisture dots my lashes, wells long dry with no reserve to spare. And so I face it. Head strong. Head long, bittersweet in priceless beauty. Where are you, love? Why do I search though you surround me? I cannot find, yet you pursue. Each moment, each minute, one step between us two. A long step. One I cannot cross and you cannot breach. Yet I feel you always. Where, love, can I find you now? Yes, right now."

Journal entry: October 23, 2018

"Pain is a funny thing. It changes us, molds us into something we ordinarily aren't. It makes us behave as though held hostage to another. As now, when I hurt too bad to write."

Journal entry: November 9, 2018

"If I were an ocean wave, I would roll along during the golden hour so I could wash the shore in champagne. If I were a breeze, I'd blow through the treetops, tickling every yellow leaf and picking the red ones to carry them along my journey. If I were a cloud, I'd wait till the evening hues could paint my body over in peace and splendor.

"But I am a man.

"And I cannot find my place today. And so I watch with awe as others around me do just what they are meant to do. To be. To really be."

As I mentioned, I was shell-shocked and felt like Joseph who was just tossed into prison with no warning. I have often read the passage I cited at the beginning of this chapter. How hard it would have been for him. Joseph didn't ask for any of his problems. He didn't do anything to deserve them. He was an innocent man, only obeying what his father had told him to do. He didn't feed the resentment his brothers had toward him. He didn't make up his dreams, in fact, they were from God himself.

If I close my eyes, I can see Joseph, hear him calling out to his Maker in the dark of the night. "What's up with this, God? Why am I here after following you so faithfully? Why have you pursued me so, letting one bad thing after another chase me down?" The whys and hows would have haunted him relentlessly. How difficult it would be to accept. Joseph was innocently thrown into prison. To add insult to injury, he was then sold to a far-away pagan country and culture. I'm sure he faced many of the same questions that you and I might face.

When I was similarly thrown into a mental prison of depression, I wondered how and why I had gotten to this place. I didn't do anything wrong to bring on all these afflictions. I didn't ask for them or look for them. I didn't boast of myself as some superhuman Christian, immune to any pain or suffering. All I was doing was following the Lord the best that I could, trying to obey what he wanted for me and my life.

I asked many questions and asked them often. "Why am I here? Why does it hurt so badly? When will I find relief? Where is God now? Why do I feel so far from him?" The whys plagued me and constantly bombarded my mind. Why had I lost so much? Why was my life falling apart? Why was the distance growing between my kids and me? I couldn't figure out any of this mystery called life. I was speechless, lost for words.

The only thing I had was an earnest cry to a (hopefully) merciful God.

Chapter 8
Barren, Fertile Ground

But the man who is not afraid to admit everything that he sees to be wrong with himself, and yet recognizes that he may be the object of God's love precisely because of his shortcomings, can begin to be sincere. His sincerity is based on confidence, not in his own illusions about himself, but in the endless, unfailing mercy of God.
~ Thomas Merton, *No Man Is an Island*

Men are born to sin . . . What does matter most, is not that we err, it is that we do benefit from our mistakes, that we are capable of sincere repentance, of genuine contrition.
~ Sharon Kay Penman, *The Sunne in Splendour*

The vastness of the empty field is before me, and my soul and spirit cry out through the night. There is no shelter, no covering, for all was destroyed by the swarm. As the infinite void of the ocean's horizon, deep calling unto deep, I stare over the endless plains once consumed. I wait, watching for movement. Can there yet be a sign of life in this great and mighty wasteland? Have the locusts destroyed beyond what the root can bear, to regain green life once more? Can a remnant repopulate what only hope fleeting thought might imagine? Are all dreams alike crushed to the floor with a blanket heavy of despair, or are the desolate fields left open as an opportunity for something new? Once described as a plague of the night, could it be that a dim flicker of reason might show me that in this bare void lay endless possibilities?

A great paradox arises. I span the empty field, much like the moment and time my eyes watched over the barrenness of the ocean floor. No, I will not accept this portrait of abandoned shadows. It shall not stay a place disrobed in vulnerability. I must believe that a beauty is in the future, and that though unknown, a new creation might sprout forth life here once again. I reach for a thread from the sky, something thin, yet tangible to take hold of. A silk thread hangs from the heavens, and I dare to reach out my hand to claim it. I grip the slightest string of delicate hope to hold, I dare not pull too hard. Its delicate form and intimate disguise I dare not chase or spook away, as I focus intently on it in form and fashion.

A curious mystery of sun dance breaks the heavens open and hands warmth to one small parcel of the naked field before me. Can, in fact, a small rebirth begin? My heart aches for the possibility of a dream revisited. I cling to the opened crack of sky that allows sunlight to now enter my world, warming it. Is there reason to base the setting of hope once more? I shall look into it with great fervor, as I own it deep inside.

§

"Then Job arose and tore his robe and shaved his head and fell on the ground and worshiped. And he said, 'Naked I came from my mother's womb, and naked shall I return. The Lord gave, and the Lord has taken away; blessed be the name of the Lord'" (Job 1:20–21).

Neither did I curse the Lord.

I held my stature and my integrity. I had been battered and beaten well enough, I felt. I wasn't asking for any more. The difficulties and afflictions my life had faced were more than I had ever dreamed would come my way. Job probably thought the same. He had been through enough yet still faced more.

One day, sitting in my chair for what seemed like another countless hour, the mailman brought a package to my door. *Odd*, I thought, since I had made no purchase or ordered anything that I could remember. I went to the back door and picked up the prize. It wasn't that big of a package, and curiosity prompted me to open it when I returned to my recliner. At the time, I was unaware that I was, in fact, opening a treasure chest that would change the course of my thoughts and the future of my life forever. It was a cardboard box, containing three books and a message. All three were written by a woman named Joni Eareckson Tada, and I looked them over.

I felt as though God himself had prompted someone to send them. There is no way that someone could have come up with something so brilliant on their own. God had to have whispered into the ear of the person who sent these gifts. It was too perfect to be a coincidence.

Jumping right into the pages of my new reads, I discovered that Joni Eareckson Tada had been in a swimming accident when her spinal column was injured, resulting in permanent paralysis in all four limbs. I read about her struggles, about her depression. I read about how she felt and saw how closely her story resembled my own feelings and thoughts. I read how she reached conclusions that positively enhanced her as a person and as a Christian. I read the pages of how God took an unfortunate situation and turned it around to be used as a witness and a ministry. I saw how God used her, even in her weakness. In a profound way, I began to see that in that exact weakness, God could be wonderfully strong in her life. As I plunged into the words penned by a woman who was paralyzed from the neck down, everything began to change.

A hard outer shell of ice was melting, allowing my heart to beat again for the first time in almost two decades. I couldn't have received a more fitting word. As the ice and snow dissolved inside me, my entire outlook and perspective on everything changed and transformed inside me. For the first time since my accident, I now saw that God could possibly take this unfortunate situation I found myself in and turn it around, bringing glory to himself. Was it possible that the same thing that happened to Joni could happen to me as well? Could my weakest moment be used to light a fire inside someone else and bring God glory? Could God take what had happened to me and use it for the furthering of his kingdom and the advancement of his name? Curiosity sparked a fire inside me—a fire to learn the answers to these burning questions.

Journal entry: November 14, 2018

"If this book is true and God works our sufferings for our benefit and for his own, then what unseen benefit is my life bringing in the making? What can my carnal eyes not see that God is doing? My God, who with unconditional everlasting love unbridled, is allowing the most tormenting things to occur to me. His hands either hold or let happen all that befalls to mankind, yet what eternal significance can I not see? What purpose is hidden from my eyes that this life of hardships will bring forth? One day, will I look back to see with understanding. Can these mountains, deserts, and valleys bring glory to my Maker? Oh, as the psalmist pens, "And I say, 'Oh, that I had wings like a dove! I would fly away and be at rest" (Psalm 55:6). But escape may rob and steal me of my greater worth and glory. Should I pass these trials, what awaits me? Oh Lord, do it well. Do it well, Lord. Be pleased with me!"

§

I now see the light of day piercing through the night. It illuminates the world I unfortunately find myself in. Bright light reveals just how far I am off course and just how far I am from finishing the trek through this barren wilderness valley. The daylight piercing through clouded skies reveals the signs around me, and I now can see plainly the mermaids who have crept upon me, disguised, devouring my flesh to consume me by permission. I care not to entertain their fancies anymore. "Enough," I say and stand to my feet once again in self-respect and dignity. With intentional muscle, I turn around and regroup. My face now points in the right direction. Casting off the mermaid-like parasites that cling to each of my sides, I break free. I shake off their sharp clawed grips. Crying out, they fall beneath me. Not enough is my freedom and my newfound stance in solid truth, I trample those beautiful snares of death named mermaids under foot. I shall not succumb to such a fate. My course lies ahead. I cannot allow the subtle sighs of unmet promise distract me from my goal. Repentance calls me loud and clear. The prize lies ahead, and I see that no affliction, light or heavy, can keep me from the end. I shall pursue; I shall move on. This field called life cannot stay barren forever.

§

At this time in my life, I began to get serious with the Lord in a new way. I was tired of playing games and dancing around the issue of who and what my life was meant to be. I was tired of wasting time and of living my days without purpose. I wasn't getting any younger. I had the opportunity of a lifetime before me, and I wasn't about to waste it. God had come to my front door, and I didn't know how long he would stand there and wait for me to run with this chance.

I sensed the urgency of his call. I could hear both his voice and his knocking on the wooden door of my heart. What was I to do now? Surely he knew me in my weakness. Surely he could identify with my condition. I felt the desire God had for me. Though broken, I could please him in my weakness. I could do nothing except be transparent, and that was the exact place that I could truly face God in both awe and repentance. With this realization, I knew it was exactly what I should do. God was God. I am only me, and with me came great shortcomings.

Repentance. What a word. A word attached and fixed firm to action. A word with intention, purpose, and drive. In its essence and simplest form, it means changing direction from one path to another. With this newfound illumination of where my life was heading came the crystal-clear understanding that I had to get off the wrong path and onto the right track before it was too late. The false promises spoken from mermaid lips couldn't satisfy me any longer. I needed to get my life on a true course. I needed to adjust my sails and trim them for action. I needed to catch hold of this new breath of life and hang on to it for all I could.

This began with my eyes opening. I knew the Lord *would not* and *could not* be pleased with how I was coping with pain. I had to change. I had to repent. Like Job, I had sat scraping my skin of loathsome disease. I could now see that I was trusting in the soothing feel of the broken pottery that I used to bring my blisters and rash relief instead of trusting in the one who could deliver me from the potter's field. It was time to let Jesus do the driving. It was time to stand and let him be the one to heal my sores.

"The heavens will not be filled with those who never made mistakes but with those who recognized that they were off course and who corrected their ways to get back in the light of gospel truth." ~ Dieter F. Uchtdorf[13]

"If you are renewed by grace, and were to meet your old self, I am sure you would be very anxious to get out of his company." ~ Charles H. Spurgeon[14]

With the revolutionary wake-up call I received from the prompting of the Holy Spirit and the books that had come in the mail, true repentance took place. It was then and only then that my whole worldview was properly changed and corrected. Everywhere I looked, life became different. My opinion and take away from my accident was radically challenged and changed. No more did I see myself as handicapped or disabled.

Instead, I began a list in my mind—and on paper too—of the things that I still *could* do instead of focusing on what had been taken away. I actually found a pen and wrote that list out one day, and the number of things that I felt I was still willing and capable of doing began to inspire me. It was pretty exciting to read a list of my still-functioning skills, despite my condition.

The creative side of my mind—I'm right-brained—still worked well. Maybe I could allow the creative juices to flow and still be productive at something. I might have had to tweak or change the media of expression, but I could still create, a deep passion of mine. I could still write, which I loved, even bound to a chair. I had started writing journal entries back when my first wife was diagnosed with cancer in 2006. Since then, I have filled many books with my thoughts. For many years, I followed through with writing with a fervor almost every day. Even in my deep despair, I had many pages full of thoughts that I felt worthy to pen.

I also felt I could still minister to people. Most people need help, often when others cannot conveniently do so. I have never really been a friend of the clock, and now my eyes were opened to see an awesome new opportunity. My whole life, I had been a slave to the clock and calendar, forced to work around a specific schedule. Now I had a wide open schedule with almost endless time for ministry that I didn't have before. No longer was this defeated Christian man limited by a schedule or bound to time the way I used to be. People who needed a listening ear could reach me at any hour of the day or night. I had no schedule. Night was the same as day to me, so it didn't matter how late someone needed encouragement. I also realized that I could pray. I was bound to a chair. If so, why not use my time to pray for other people? With these new purposes, my lungs filled and breathed again. I felt as though each day I was becoming a new man. I was transforming. My life would change and never be the same.

Depression ceased, as I became fueled with purpose to allow God to use me as a broken vessel. I opened myself up to the possibility that he could use me *as is*, which was vitally important. I didn't need to go to school to get another degree. No requirements needed to be met. All too often, Christians think that they have to gain credentials before the Lord can use them. Let me tell you that God *can* and *will* use you *as is* if you allow him to do so. Yes, I stood as an injured man. But now I knew that he was actually using me for something far greater than I could have imagined, and I needed nothing more to be ready for this cause. Could the Lord make a better me post-accident? Could he still use me, even with the perceived permanent injury of my ear and the crazy amount of time that I was required to sit still in a chair during the day? My willingness to be used was the only thing God asked of me.

"Then Job answered the Lord and said:
'I know that you can do all things,
and that no purpose of yours can be thwarted.
Who is this that hides counsel without knowledge?'
Therefore I have uttered what I did not understand,
things too wonderful for me, which I did not know.
"Hear, and I will speak;
I will question you, and you make it known to me."
I had heard of you by the hearing of the ear,
but now my eye sees you;
therefore I despise myself,
and repent in dust and ashes'" (Job 42:1–6).

Chapter 9
God's Sovereignty, Our Responsibility

It is better to light a candle than curse the darkness.
~ Eleanor Roosevelt

I look to the heavens. I declare my integrity is just. A curse not invited, a nightmare not provoked, I certainly never asked for my life to be like this. How, then, does depression cloak my mind with my surroundings scattered in disarray? In what way have I brought these plagues upon myself? When did I cry to the locust to devour my life? When was a messenger sent to the blackness of despair? How have the words of my lips played the Pied Piper's song of destruction, bringing it to my doorstep? When did I allow my life to be laid waste?

I stand before my Father as a cracked and broken vessel. The same man that once was used to store the words that God brought to so many others now cannot even hold the base and simple foundations of life

192

together. Altogether bruised and broken, I lie dormant, cracked, shattered into pieces that I cannot form together. Life has drained the sap from my living fibers. I no longer look to be anything at all.

A form fallen, a man made of rust, my name no longer holds the luster of the one I once brightly beamed for. My light is diffused and darkened; it smolders as a flame about to extinguish. Can this vessel still be used? Are these broken pieces a puzzle too damaged for God to build again? To restore? Why, Lord? What purpose has this evil swarm produced in me?

In my frustration, words escape from the tongue I wish to silence. How I wish to retract them again. Who am I to pose such a question of stupidity? The Lord thunders a mighty hand upon me. I shudder in his presence. At a moment's notice, the sky and heavens flee before him, as all obey the plan and purpose of his voice. Yet do I? Is the one created justified before the Creator? I certainly must hope he is a merciful God. I lie before him. I am in the wrong. The Lord can use a broken man best, and so broken I shall be.

§

What shall we say then? Is there injustice on God's part? By no means! For he says to Moses, "I will have mercy on whom I have mercy, and I will have compassion on whom I have compassion." So then it depends not on human will or exertion, but on God, who has mercy. For

193

the Scripture says to Pharaoh, "For this very purpose I have raised you up, that I might show my power in you, and that my name might be proclaimed in all the earth." So then he has mercy on whomever he wills, and he hardens whomever he wills.

You will say to me then, "Why does he still find fault? For who can resist his will?" But who are you, O man, to answer back to God? Will what is molded say to its molder, "Why have you made me like this?" Has the potter no right over the clay, to make out of the same lump one vessel for honorable use and another for dishonorable use? (Romans 9:14–21)

This, a very curious time period in my life, began to bloom. It seemed as though I was learning a very important lesson, one that I hope not to soon forget. Could it be that I would have any plea or word in edgewise with the Lord himself? Certainly not. I began to see how foolish a thought like that looked now.

In all reality, God certainly did have my life in his hands. I know the old Sunday School song we used to sing as little children, "He's Got the Whole World in His Hands." Did I really believe it?

To have the beautiful valley of delight and pleasure that I walked in during my early twenties turn into the barren wasteland of my thirties and forties, well, this simply didn't make any sense to the soul who never stopped believing and following the Lord. Did I have a right to be angry?

I did become angry. Deep down, I'm not sure that it would have been humanly possible to experience what I had lived through without some type of resentment toward the Lord. I watched my first wife suffer with an extremely rare case of stomach cancer for someone her age. I watched her body deteriorate until she finally passed away to be with the Lord, even after all my faith and prayers. I watched my church and church family, those I had grown up with, lived with, and spent time with for my entire life self-destruct and fall apart right before my eyes. I watched the ministry that I worked so earnestly for and had put so much effort into dissolve. I felt betrayed by others—church leaders and even friends.

I trusted the Lord when he brought me a new love and the promise of a happy family again. I thought all would now be perfect, but I could not keep life from crumbling internally once more. I faced grieving the broken dream of another marriage when it was unhealthy for that marriage to continue. I missed the company that I once had. I faced the separation from my stepchildren, though I loved them, and grieved being apart from them as well. After a serious accident, my skull was cracked in two places, and I faced permanent hearing loss and other long-term disabilities. I faced the difficulty of grieving a second time for my first wife. I knew what it felt like to be depressed, lonely, and helpless. I had been reduced to nothing.

Yes, I was angry.

And then, my perspective drastically changed. "Then the Lord answered Job out of the whirlwind and said: 'Dress for action like a man; I will question you, and you make it known to me. Will you even put me in the wrong? Will you condemn me that you may be in the right? Have you an arm like God, and can you thunder with a voice like his?'" (Job 40:6–9).

Who was I to speak a word against the Lord?

Ultimately, God is in control. We can either fight or embrace this universal law. Regardless of our stance on the matter, the statement is still true. The Lord *was* always and *will* always be in control of my life and the circumstances that I find myself in. Was God in control in my life even when hardships came? Yes. Could I believe it? Maybe.

To arrive at such a conclusion, you might need to reach rock bottom. So often in life, you might say those words, almost as if you flippantly utter a cheap cliché of inspirational meanings. Alcoholics Anonymous uses the term in the therapy they provide. Other rehabilitation groups and services know the familiarity of the phrase as well. Songs are even sung about hitting rock bottom. Is this a fun place to be? In the lowest point possible, what can we learn once we arrive there? Do we really believe and trust that God "has the whole world in his hands," like the song says? Are we willing, as Job, to accept both the good *and* the evil that life brings us? Do we really accept those things? To really and truly accept what the Lord allows to befall us, well, that's a different story altogether.

With my newfound epiphany, I began to examine the truth of the matter. Whether or not I *enjoyed* what life handed me was not conditional on the truth that God had allowed me to live it. Quite honestly, I realized that my take on the matter really didn't count. Being happy or bent out of shape about it was not conditional on what God did or did not do. I began to see that just because something is not fun, enjoyable, or even likable has no real merit to the way life will go. The Lord is an all-knowing God. He is our heavenly Father. We don't always have to like what he does. Sometimes a dad knows what he is doing even when a child cannot see it. Could my heavenly Father have something up his sleeve that I was not aware of?

Slowly but surely, my eyes were really opened. I weighed it all and stood back to take a good look. My conclusion was this: God does not cause harm to his children. He is too good to do that. God does not go around zapping people with plagues to make them better and stronger in ministry. He does not cut legs off to make souls tougher and stronger. He doesn't kill people to make the survivors appreciate life more. He's not like that.

But—and I cannot scream the word *but* loudly enough—"And we know that for those who love God all things work together for good, for those who are called according to his purpose" (Romans 8:28).

Romans 8:28 has become my motto. In the book of Romans, we clearly see the nature and character of our loving Father. We live in a fallen world ever since Adam and Eve bit into that forbidden fruit. Bad things happen, period. Evil surrounds us in a fallen world. The beautiful thing is that God promises to be true to his own nature and be *good*, even when those bad things happen. He simply cannot be anything but good. In his goodness, he takes the effects of a fallen world of sin and turns those around for his glory and our benefit. He *is* in control, even when we, as mankind, go our own selfish ways. We live each and every day with the consequences of the fall of mankind when we sinned in the garden of Eden. God, however, is too good to let sin reign.

With the newfound and solid knowledge that God ultimately *is* in control, I began to seek and search what a good God might want to do in me. I became aware, through the wise advice of one of my life coaches, that all I needed to do was obey God each day, one step at a time. I didn't need the big plan all at once; I just needed to obey what he showed me on a daily basis.

That is exactly what I set out to do.

My perspective was changed.

Journal entry: October 6, 2018

"It is amazing what a soul takes for granted each day. Day by day, night by night, daunting, the ever-present tasks of the American way or perhaps the human way cloaked in American disguise. And so, as ants marching strong to the beat others play, we rush our mighty agendas to shore and wave their colors, beaching them as monuments of the only important thing the sun has yet to see. And yet, this roar of silence stops from time to time, for those most fortunate to sneak a breath in edgewise have the clearer sight that nothing is actually beached there, standing tall to begin with—all sand sculptures, prizes in the winds, melodies of tunes not written down. And so the question begs, the pangs inside pull for answers as providential happenstance has paused your tuned and waiting ear. What is the most important aspect? Where does your treasure lie? It won't make a bit of difference unless you place it in his skies."

Journal entry: November 16, 2018

"Everything is changing, including my perspective. God saw fit to bring this book [*A Place of Healing*] into my life, and it is changing me.

"I cannot express the gratitude I feel after becoming aware of what my Savior is doing. I am so grateful for my suffering. I am so grateful for my accident. For without it, I would be walking the same path. Searching. Empty.

"But now I see something very exciting.

"God very much had the chance to take me home. I was even ready. I was at peace to go.

"But he didn't take me.

"And if he didn't take me, then he has a reason for not doing so. And if he has a reason, then I have a purpose. I have a purpose.

"I have a purpose.

"I may not know what it is yet, but it's there. And that is wonderful news.

"Lord, please continue. Please show me in your timing what you have chosen for me to do, to be, to bring you glory."

A profound mystery began to occur that I still see as amazing to this day. I have looked back in my journals over the years. A common theme weaves a silver lining through all of them—the fact that, through all these years, I felt as if I were searching, scratching, and reaching for purpose. I was a little bitty fish in a big old world. For *years*, I craved purpose. I was starving for it. I desired purpose for my life above all the other tasks and jobs that life handed me. I was never satisfied, never full.

This has been a constant voice in the back of my head and mind, reminding me that my life needs to be used for something of greater good. Considering that I am an ENFP, this all makes considerable sense.[15] I'm wired to think in terms of purpose and passion. But regardless of my personality, my life must have purpose, something higher than myself. I was convinced of it. No matter who or what told me otherwise, I would not and could not be satisfied simply living life for myself. Surely, I had purpose. Surely, my purpose wasn't all used up in the past, and now I was a spent, smoking round. Surely, I was not supposed to walk in this wilderness forever. Surely, the good Lord had created me for a reason, right?

I realized that I had been starving to make a difference. I didn't want my life to go up in smoke when Christ judges the impact of our lives in this world (1

Corinthians 3:13–15). Rather I desperately wanted to hear the words, "well done, good and faithful servant" and be ushered into glory with a proud Father who was pleased with my life. I wanted to hear that I had obeyed the Lord and used my life for the exact reason he had formed it. I wanted to accomplish and fulfill the reason and purpose that God had breathed life into my lungs for.

But I never knew what it was.

Now beauty bathed my whole situation in a blanket of promise. Through the pain my life endured, God was focusing my eyesight and fine-tuning my skills so that I could be used effectively for the exact purpose I had been searching for.

It was beyond beautiful when I finally looked at it that way.

It still amazes me.

Chapter 10
Goodness Higher Than Ours

Life is either a daring adventure or nothing at all.
~ Helen Keller

It is in your broken places you are most often used by God.
~ Christine Caine

I search it out, yet I know not what I am to become. The future of my life lies quiet, wrapped in secret and great mystery. My days are numbered, yet I know not their value or tally. Blindly, I walk down a path unknown to anyone but the Maker of them all. He has written my script, and I read it promptly on cue, without knowing the next line.

Though unaware of what lies ahead, I grasp the hand that desires to lead me. Though a dark glass shows only dimly lit figures of the future me, I cling to the one who created me, for he knows each step I am destined to walk, to take. Should the foot formed resist walking the path paved for it to travel? Should I, in feeble knowledge, think myself better than the one whose plan was made before the dawn of time began?

In the mere understanding of the now, I am contained. The mere glimpse of the moment is the only thing I comprehend, and that, with eyes unfocused, unclear. Should I accept the plan the Creator has blueprinted for my life? There is no satisfaction in anything more or less than that. What could I possibly accomplish in life that could light a candle to the plan and purpose God has in store for me? May I achieve that which my Creator has preplanned. To God be the glory, and it is well with my soul.

§

I again want to propose a question to myself, one that I've already thought long, deep, and hard about. Would I have ever learned these truths if not for the afflictions I faced? Would my eyes ever have been opened to the mystery of these things, save for sufferings that God could turn around and teach me something with? God knows me for sure.

I can be stubborn and thickskulled, which shows how hard of a hit it took to fracture me in my accident. I have the tendency to learn things the hard way. A friend often tells me that "God is using a hammer to teach you again." It is by far easier for someone else to see what is going on in my life than for me to be self-aware. I have contemplated this long and hard and have come to a conclusion.

If it weren't for getting hit on the head, I never would have slowed down enough to hear God, to listen to the gentle whisper of our Lord's voice. I was a man on a mission, but it just wasn't the mission God had planned for me. Without the injury, I can safely say I never would have slowed down to give him the chance or even the time of day.

I can see that for sure in my journal entries and in other things that I've written over the years. I was living in a cycle of dissatisfaction while searching for purpose, discontented with the life of a typical American, with a normal job, a paycheck, and a schedule I was enslaved to. I wanted and craved more. Sadly, I know I never would have come to the place to receive more without this blessing in disguise.

I have told many people, "My accident is the best thing that has ever happened to me." Most people might not believe that, but I truly believe that, aside from the decision I made to accept Christ as my Savior, nothing has topped the hit on the head that changed my life forever. I hope it doesn't stop there. I hope my life continues to move forward in the adjustment that he has redirected me in. I hope my life affects many others as I start on a course to help hurting people. This experience has undeniably changed everything about me. It may consequently also change yours.

The devil never gets the upper hand over the Lord. God can turn the most negative experience into something that will produce fruit for him and his kingdom. If you allow him to, God *can* and *will* do it in your life as well.

Journal entry: November 17, 2018

"I've decided to let God shine through my cracks. I'm a broken vessel. But I'm still a vessel. Yesterday, I bought the book for [a hurting friend] who needs to hear these truths as much as I did. I'm convinced that this accident I've had and the suffering I've gone through is only one more qualification on my resume, one more tool in my box, one more arrow to diversify my quiver. Should God see fit, I can be used in even more ways now. Praise be to his name. He is glorified even more.

"Consequently—and I'm not sure if I've written about this yet or not in this journal—I'm actually almost glad. I know that sounds odd. But what is better: light shining out of a broken vessel's crack, or no light shining at all because the vessel has no cracks for the light to escape through? May I be able to do something, somewhere, at some time to let that light shine to aid someone else to become closer to the Lord and to glorify his name."

> O Lord, you have searched me and known me!
> You know when I sit down and when I rise up;
> you discern my thoughts from afar.
> You search out my path and my lying down
> and are acquainted with all my ways.
> Even before a word is on my tongue,
> behold, O Lord, you know it altogether.
> You hem me in, behind and before,
> and lay your hand upon me.

Such knowledge is too wonderful for me;
it is high; I cannot attain it.
Where shall I go from your Spirit?
Or where shall I flee from your presence?
If I ascend to heaven, you are there!
If I make my bed in Sheol, you are there!
If I take the wings of the morning
and dwell in the uttermost parts of the sea,
even there your hand shall lead me,
and your right hand shall hold me.
If I say, "Surely the darkness shall cover me,
and the light about me be night,"
even the darkness is not dark to you;
the night is bright as the day,
for darkness is as light with you.
For you formed my inward parts;
you knitted me together in my mother's womb.
I praise you, for I am fearfully and wonderfully
made.
Wonderful are your works;
my soul knows it very well.
My frame was not hidden from you,
when I was being made in secret,
intricately woven in the depths of the earth.
Your eyes saw my unformed substance;
in your book were written, every one of them,
the days that were formed for me,
when as yet there was none of them.
How precious to me are your thoughts, O God!
How vast is the sum of them!
If I would count them, they are more than the
sand.
I awake, and I am still with you. (Psalm 139:1–
18)

Does the Lord care for a man such as me? Does he have a plan for my life more intricate than I could ever imagine or comprehend? Psalm 139 gives us just a hint and inkling about how the Lord has put an almost infinite amount of care and attention into forming us and the plan he has for our lives. We are curiously made in the most precise and perfect way, even in what we might not understand about ourselves. There is nothing hidden or unknown to the Lord. He knows you and your creative makeup even better than you know yourself, for he is the one who has built and made you.

He not only designed each cell of your body, your genetic makeup, and the intangible parts of you, such as your personality, but he has also designed and planned out all your days. He knows exactly why you have been created the way you are. It is beautiful to him, for he made you specifically the way he did for a reason. Our ultimate goal in life is to achieve that fulfillment. To live the life that he has purposed for us to live and fulfill the days that he has planned for us would be the ultimate satisfaction when we meet him face to face. He knew our exact purpose even before the beginning of time, and he destined you for a specific reason.

"How precious to me are your thoughts, O God! How vast the sum of them! If I would count them, they are more than the sand. I awake, and I am still with you." How divinely precious are those words! The Creator of the entire universe, who has everything in his hands to care for, has little old me in mind that much. Simply unfathomable! How much higher are God's ways than our ways? We will not fully grasp this until we are in heaven with him. He knows us. He made us. He sees the big picture. He has a plan that we cannot really comprehend. The only way to truly live is to just accept it for what it is.

Come, everyone who thirsts,
come to the waters;
and he who has no money,
come, buy and eat!
Come, buy wine and milk
without money and without price.
Why do you spend your money for that which is not bread,
and your labor for that which does not satisfy?
Listen diligently to me, and eat what is good,
and delight yourselves in rich food.
Incline your ear, and come to me;
hear, that your soul may live;
and I will make with you an everlasting covenant,
my steadfast, sure love for David.
Behold, I made him a witness to the peoples,
a leader and commander for the peoples.
Behold, you shall call a nation that you do not know,
and a nation that did not know you shall run to you,
because of the Lord your God, and of the Holy One of Israel,
for he has glorified you.
Seek the Lord while he may be found;
call upon him while he is near;
let the wicked forsake his way,
and the unrighteous man his thoughts;
let him return to the Lord, that he may have

compassion on him,
and to our God, for he will abundantly pardon.
For my thoughts are not your thoughts,
neither are your ways my ways, declares the Lord.
For as the heavens are higher than the earth,
so are my ways higher than your ways
and my thoughts than your thoughts. (Isaiah 55:1–9)

Journal entry: November 22. 2018

"I don't even know how to write or what to say. I'm speechless. Paralyzed in a sort of way.

"Awestruck.

"I wanted to get up and write about what 2 Corinthians 1 had spoken to me. But instead, I received a note of evidence that the Lord is, in fact, using me and doing something with me as I had hoped.

"[The friend I sent the book to] just sent me a message. It humbled me so much that I just went up to my room and lay down on the floor in worship to my King.

"God used me. And I heard his voice correctly. And sending her this book was, in fact, what the Lord wanted me to do. And she was thankful for what the Lord did through me this year as she reflected on Thanksgiving.

"I am so humbled.

"I am so thankful he used me.

"I *do* matter for something.

"I *did* matter.

"I *am* living a life of purpose.

"God was gracious enough to tell me this morning.

"I'm so thankful he let my injury happen."

Do we know his final plan? Are we as wise as the Lord himself? Of course not! We are humans, built and knit with a finite mind. An infinite God can see much further down the line than we could ever hope to. Does everything make sense to us as far as timing or from a human's eyesight and understanding, from our point of view? We would be fooling ourselves to pretend that. There is simply a great divide between God's infinite ways and our finite human understanding.

"You have kept count of my tossings; put my tears in your bottle. Are they not in your book?" (Psalm 56:8). Okay. It's time for me to be transparent. This Scripture baffles me. I cannot wrap my hands around this passage. Why, might one ask, would God want to keep count of my tossings? What does that even mean?

To read those words now, looking back at all the chaos and agony that I have endured through the last fifteen years, I hardly can put together my thoughts or wrap my arms around what God's Word actually says. Some nights, I cried myself to sleep, even blaming God in part, or, at least, pinning the permission for this affliction on him. If that is how I felt, how could he love me in such a way that he would still care for me this intensely? In fact, how could he possibly record all the nights that I spent roaming all over the bed with very little sleep for fifteen years? They were so many. Doesn't he have so many other things to do?

The restless nights were more than I could even count. I spent so many nights tossing in this manner, more than I recorded in my journals, more than I can tell. How could he begin to keep track or watch the progression of all those nights I spent, the nights I couldn't sleep at all? Why would he care? Seriously? I went through hell, and now, you mean to tell me that the Lord was watching me closely enough to keep track of all those sleepless nights? How amazing it is to realize that God was right there with me, even though I couldn't see.

God, did you really put my tears in your bottle?

I know what it means to keep things in a bottle. I am a very sentimental man. I prefer personal keepsakes that mean something to me as opposed to a purchased item from a store. I keep seashells from each and every beach I go to around the world. I have countless bottles at home that keep priceless mementos safe, taken from trips and adventures I've gone on. I have a bottle of pink sand from Bermuda, a shiny bottle of glittery sand from Lake Tahoe, a bottle with white sand from the Florida Keys, and a very nice bottle of sand from the Amazon River bank in Iniridia, Columbia. I have collections of shells and sea glass from all over the western world from Bermuda to California, Maine to South America. All my bottles of shells and sand are special to me. I look at them from time to time and think of the memories that I have stored from the beaches of each of those places. I leave a little part of me on each sandy shore. I smile at the thought and memory of what all my bottles represent.

God, how this verse touches me. In light of this, do you mean to tell me that you keep my tears in your bottle? Are my sorrows, tears, and moments of such sadness special enough to you that you would want to keep them, treasure them, and remember them? What purpose do these things serve? I cannot fathom or explain this profound love that God has for me. Yes, the God of the universe puts something of *me* in his bottles. Not only that, but my *tears*, of all things? Why? Why would God hold my tears closer to himself than anything else about me?

Perhaps I'm the closest to my Father in the moments spent in tears.

His bottle stores the reminders of our best times together.

When I set out to obey the Lord each and every day for what it was, my life began to transform right before my eyes. The most curious of things began to happen. I'm not sure I can explain it, yet I'll give it my best.

I woke up each day with the attitude to obey the God that created me and had me in his hands. I put in the time to get to know him better. I was in his Word and in serious prayer time with him. I began talking to him once more in an incredibly intimate way. My prayer time became one of the most important moments of my day.

Each night, I went to bed early after I took care of whatever I needed to. I knelt beside my bed and simply talked to God. It was amazing how time passed. It wasn't a burden to pray for needs or to sacrifice my time in prayer. No, on the contrary, I was enjoying my time with God, and his "banner was over me [was] love" (Song of Solomon 2:4).

The nights that I spent in prayer slowly showed me evidence that the Lord was enjoying my company with him as well. We shared so many wonderful moments together. Although I was still injured and still alone most of the day, an interesting thing began to happen, something that I had battled to reach and obtain my entire life. I realized that I had acquired a priceless treasure through this entire process, a tremendous gift. Sadly, most other people never receive this quality in life.

I became content.

Society fights tooth and nail against the virtue of contentment. It goes against everything we know and the current American way. We tear down lovely houses to build bigger and better ones. We sell cars that still work to buy faster ones and with newer upgrades. Our culture loves the next model, the next big thing. A customer might be satisfied with the latest iPhone today, only to treat it like an obsolete item of embarrassment a short two years down the road when the contract term is up. We simply must get that next thing. We are constantly pursuing something new. The nature of society breeds dissatisfaction in what we have, turning grateful hearts and lives into craving what we do not possess. We are never happy with what we have, continually climbing a ladder, in a constant rat race we never complete. Our culture is rarely, if ever, content.

Yet here, in my brokenness and pain, in my attachment to living in a chair all day and all week, I found something new and priceless. Through all the pain my head battled with, through all the heartache my heart and insides fought through the last fifteen years, through all the scars, even through the permanent hearing impairment in my left ear, along with the crazy loud and constant ringing, something peculiar budded and formed.

I found myself enjoying contentment.

The mystery of contentment is not found in social status. The world will never find contentment in money or riches. Fame never satisfies those who chase it. Even power loses its luster once people reach the top. King Solomon must have thought that a special woman would finally bring him contentment, but after marrying three thousand of them, he still wrote in the book of Ecclesiastes with the pen of a dissatisfied man. He concluded that "everything is meaningless."

I personally thought that a man must have a woman to hold on his arm to be content. I was so lonely. My solitude had gotten the best of me, and I was tired of feeling miserable. Day after day, I felt I had to find a woman to complete me. I figured if I had a companion, my pain and troubles would be eased. This was far from the truth.

I discovered that in my sweet times when praying with the Lord in a room only he and I shared, I felt complete. The Lord began to complete me in ways I never dreamed he could or would. He was a companion sweeter than any other. He never left my side. In my pain, he understood. In the frustration of my ringing ear, he never forgot his gentle hold on me. In the night, when I couldn't sleep, he was always open for a chat. He provided such a satisfaction inside me that a relationship with a woman simply couldn't compare. My focus switched off my situation.

Slowly, things changed. It didn't matter to me if I was single or not. What mattered more was that I was now in right standing with the Lord and that God was truly in charge. I was satisfied with what he had given me. In my situation, this was not a sudden light switch that flipped on but a progression. Over the next few weeks and months, the satisfaction I had and my confidence that God was in control of me and my life became so stable and peaceful. I didn't mind my deaf ear anymore. I saw it as special. I didn't mind that I couldn't stand to do activities that I enjoyed anymore, such as painting, working, and playing with the kids. I found that I was still very capable of doing other important and essential things, even from my chair.

"What shall I say? For he has spoken to me, and he himself has done it. I walk slowly all my years because of the bitterness of my soul. O Lord, by these things men live, and in all these is the life of my spirit. Oh restore me to health and make me live!" (Isaiah 38:15–16). That is exactly what began to glow inside me. I became happy and content in my situation. I treasure this as you cannot buy it. It was a pleasure.

Looking back, I can see how silly I was. During the single and miserable time of my life, I spent way too much energy focusing on what I didn't have. I was so stupid to think that stressing and focusing on it would help. I used to watch movies with actresses that I knew to be single, admiring them as if I were personally getting to know them or were able to ask them out. I listened to music sung and written by single female artists as if I had a chance to actually date them. As silly as it sounds, I even looked up how old they were to see if we might make a compatible match. One night, I even photo-shopped a picture of Shakira next to me, sending it to my siblings in a text with a caption that read, "save the date." I was a hopeless romantic and hopelessly depressed. It was silly but true. I cannot state how grateful I am that the Lord had enough compassion to reach down and teach me how to be content in my situation. I was not in a pretty place.

Journal entry: December 9, 2018

"So the Lord is teaching me. Maybe I am just now letting him; I don't know. But I finished my book last night. I think I'm learning something that you can't teach others. Contentment is an acquired gift. Some fairy godmother can't tap you on the head and tell you, 'Now you have contentment.'

"No, this gift can only be received through fire and storms. For when the hurricane has passed, the one who possesses nothing has acquired the best thing of all: contentment.

"In a nutshell, Joni Eareckson Tada says in her book that when we totally and completely trust God's plan for our now—even singleness—without fear of the unknown, then this removes the worry, fear, and bitterness. Once you accept it, it doesn't matter anymore. If you stay single or if God brings you someone down the road, either way, you are in God's plan, and you are content.

"It was such a great book. So what is my now?

"Well, I am learning how to live joyfully single. And God is walking with me as he trains and teaches me. I can't go wrong.

"My now is a pirate life. Two boys are sleeping in their bedrooms, and I just found [Brad's friend] sleeping on a couch downstairs. My now is a life of tilling soil in their lives and hearts. My now is possibly a foundation for a future. But even if God chooses to keep me here, he is bringing people into my life who need a hand and a prayer.

"Praise God for where I am.

"I've been told over and over, 'Why do you have to do something *big* for the Lord? Why can't you just be happy living? Why do you chase purpose?' Well, tonight I thought about those voices in my head again. But you know what? What does it matter? Let them talk. Let them laugh. Let them think I'm an idiot.

"I simply don't want to lead an ordinary life. I *want* God to do something *extraordinary* with me. I'm not satisfied with just living. I want to be used by him.

"I pray my prayer is answered."

Would God leave me there? I wasn't sure. But I knew for certain that he was holding me, and that was more important. Oddly enough, at that time, we needed to start preparing for a mission trip that had been planned and scheduled long before my accident occurred.

We had planned in August to take a trip to go visit close missionary friends living in Bogotá, Colombia. Even before the days when we taught the youth group so long ago, my family was very involved with missions in the Amazon River basin of South America. I had been in contact with and supported an amazing couple for the past twenty years. Our relationship was mutually beneficial, and the interaction we cherished was blessing both the Amazon River basin and western Pennsylvania. They had put me in touch with a fantastic husband-and-wife team in Colombia who were on fire for the Lord, and we began supporting them as well. For years, I dreamed of seeing the work that we supported with my own eyes. I didn't just want to hear about updates or look at online pictures of what the Lord was doing in the jungle. I wanted to actually see it, feel it, and live it.

The purchase of non-refundable tickets in August meant we could not turn back. September had unexpectedly brought my accident. Although I was really struggling with my health, I didn't want to back out of the trip. It was too important to me. When I brought this up to my medical and rehabilitation team, all my therapists and doctors told me the same thing. They thought the entire trip would be too difficult for me in my condition and counseled against it. They all advised me against this trip of a lifetime. They felt that with a traumatic brain injury, the trip would simply be too much: the rush and chaos of airports, the culture change, another language that my brain would have to switch to, the long trips and connections, the busy pace of travel. The doctors and professionals felt I wouldn't be able to process information and stimuli. I would then become overloaded, confused, and unstable. My dream was to be there, though, so a very difficult decision needed to be made.

Sometimes the right thing to do is the most difficult choice, and the right choice involves the most work. Sometimes the enemy might be trying to discourage us from following through with what the Lord has in store. Sometimes you have to go with what God is whispering to you, the thing that you can feel in your spirit.

Against the doctor and therapist's advice, I told them I was doing it. I wouldn't budge on my plans. Instead of convincing me that I wouldn't be able to handle certain things, I told them to change their thinking and to get me ready for what I would face. They complied. It was very hard work.

I had a brain injury and had to brush up on my Spanish and successfully navigate foreign airports with no English-speaking people. Let's just say the bar was raised quite high. God himself would need to prepare me.

I worked hard with my Rosetta Stone software and practiced daily. I knew Spanish well enough, but I was not sure if my injured brain could recall words and phrases and switch over to a second language at the drop of a hat. I tried to make mental lists of what we would need. With extreme difficulty, I filled out forms and papers. Slowly and surely, we were able to update passports and get the immunizations necessary to travel to the Amazon lowlands. It was very challenging work for someone who couldn't even drive a car at the time. But the Lord was with me.

The trip happened. To say that I was blown away spiritually was a total understatement. I wasn't just blown away; I was completely floored and humbled beyond measure. I was taken to a place inside my own soul that showed me how incredibly intricate God's hand is in our lives. He has everything in his control, and he knows what he is doing. I came away from the trip totally humbled beyond what I could contain, as I saw how the Lord links and networks people from distant lands and cultures to do his work and how personal his touch is.

People I had never met before showed up from miles around just to meet the three of us who were working alongside them in this Great Commission initiative. People with no money and no means somehow made a way to travel for days, in some cases, up or down the river to meet their mission partners. How does one travel a three-day journey without any money? I may never know. These people, however, figured out how to come and meet their brothers in Christ who showed up in their own jungle village, a place with no way in and no way out, except by plane, and surrounded by the thick, dense Colombian rainforest. The difficult travel situation did not keep a North American from making the trip. It wouldn't prevent the indigenous tribal brothers and sisters from making their way to meet us either. Both parties were tenaciously determined.

My visit to Colombia really refocused my vision in the grand scheme of life. What I did back in Pennsylvania clearly was making a big difference in a culture worlds away. I even had the chance to speak in a Sunday church service there. I felt like the most privileged person in the world. How many others have the chance to speak in a small village with no cars, chain restaurants, or traffic lights? In that moment, I had everybody's attention. All eyes were focused on what I had to say. You rarely have an attentive stage like that back home. There in Colombia, I had every ear.

Our missionary friend and a local indigenous church leader baptized my two sons in the waters of the Amazon River. It was a service like no other, an incredibly humbling opportunity. The whole hillside was filled with souls who wished to see their partners from America be baptized there in their own neck of the woods. I was told later, "You have no idea what that meant to each one of them. Every soul there knew that *even if they wanted to*, they could not reach the lost tribal people around them without help from people like you." They simply didn't have the materials or the means to reach the lost of the jungle. People who support missions *do* make a difference.

I could not hold back my tears.

Would the Lord leave me in a barren wasteland? That is like asking a loving and caring father if he would leave his child in a cold and lonely abandoned parking lot while he drove away. That would be unthinkable for a man. It would also be unfathomable for God.

I was being taken to much greater places. No longer did my feet walk on the dry and parched cracks of barren desert wasteland. The soft hint of something fresh and new grew beneath me. The field I walked and wandered had new promise. Yes, I was content now, but would God leave me in that place? Absolutely not. He had much more in store for me to do, and I was about to find out just how much God's hand still held for me.

Chapter 11
A Flower Blooms

*We must accept infinite disappointment, but never lose sight of
infinite hope.*
~ Martin Luther King Jr.

I am better off healed than I ever was unbroken.
~ Beth Moore

We know what we are, but know not what we may be.
~ William Shakespeare

After *two whole years*, Pharaoh dreamed that he
was standing by the Nile, and behold, there came
up out of the Nile seven cows, attractive and
plump, and they fed in the reed grass.

Then the chief cupbearer said to Pharaoh, "I
remember my offenses today. When Pharaoh was
angry with his servants and put me and the chief
baker in custody in the house of the captain of the
guard, we dreamed on the same night, he and I,

225

each having a dream with its own interpretation. A young Hebrew was there with us, a servant of the captain of the guard. When we told him, he interpreted our dreams to us, giving an interpretation to each man according to his dream. And as he interpreted to us, so it came about. I was restored to my office, and the baker was hanged."

Then Pharaoh sent and called Joseph, and they quickly brought him out of the pit. And when he had shaved himself and changed his clothes, he came in before Pharaoh. (Genesis 41:1–2, 9–14, emphasis added)

§

The gentle rain pats comfort on the skin of soil underneath the heavens. Its dry, cracked surface begs for each touch of solace received. The ground embraces the drops of the refreshing rain of life. They soak in with joy. The earth rejoices at the coming of this vital shower of grace and tranquility. I stare at the parched soil and watch it swell. Health is evidently expanding the particles and fibers within it. The cracks begin to dissipate, filling into the background tilth of organic matter present. Rich color heightens and chases each dry crack of death away. A valley once thought of with only despair now teems with the promise and aroma of earth-held fertility. Can such a place now bring forth bud? Closely watched seeds begin to swell, and the dark, rich soil releases its wealth.

Bursting forth like the ray of sunshine that preceded it, the very life and breath of the valley is birthed in a single, small green shoot. Roots are released, and by divine appointment reach for the water that heaven itself has blessed them with. They drink in the ever-satisfying taste of pureness. Revived with the drink of the skies, they fuel the expansion of growing shoots and stems. Leaves open like hands to praise the Father of creation above in thankfulness and adoration of the unforgotten care he generously provides.

And I alone stand mystified at this miracle, watching in awe.

The valley transforms into a meadow, and a clear river of crystal spring water runs through it.

§

This proposal pleased Pharaoh and all his servants. And Pharaoh said to his servants, "Can we find a man like this, in whom is the Spirit of God?" Then Pharaoh said to Joseph, "Since God has shown you all this, there is none so discerning and wise as you are. You shall be over my house, and all my people shall order themselves as you command. Only as regards the throne will I be greater than you." And Pharaoh said to Joseph, "See, I have set you over all the land of Egypt." Then Pharaoh took his signet ring from his hand and put it on Joseph's hand, and clothed him in garments of fine linen and put a gold chain about his neck. And he made him ride in his second chariot. And they called out before him, "Bow the knee!" Thus he set him over all the land of Egypt. Moreover, Pharaoh said to Joseph, "I am Pharaoh, and without your consent no one shall lift up hand or foot in all the land of Egypt." And Pharaoh called Joseph's name Zaphenath-paneah. And he gave him in marriage Asenath, the daughter of Potiphera priest of On. So Joseph went out over the land of Egypt. (Genesis 41:37–45)

Journal entry: January 7, 2019

"How do I even begin to write this entry? I don't even know where to start.

"God doesn't have to be gracious. But that's who and what he is. So I guess when we receive grace, in essence, we receive a piece of God himself. Could I have received a piece of that grace last night? My soul tossed to and fro on the ocean waves all night long. Not because of what happened but because of what could happen. I suppose that the what-ifs of life could consume a person if allowed, and I give them too much freedom.

"Last night a beautiful woman stayed up and texted with me for over an hour. It felt so incredible. It was sooo nice to talk to an adult at that hour.

"I made myself available. She needed help. But what I didn't expect was that the help she needed was the same help I needed, and it may have been just as beneficial for me as it was for her. We talked about so many things:

life, death, loss, hurt, hope, and more. Deep, yes, incredibly deep conversations.

"I daydreamed last night of what it would be like to have a woman beside me in bed. A companion. A friend. Someone close. It was incredibly nice. But I'd rather look the devil himself in the eye than at what my fears look like. At least I know the devil can't hurt me.

"She is beautiful.

"And I do like coffee."

Journal entry: January 8, 2019

"I'm not sure how to explain how I feel. The most overwhelming blessing is blossoming before my eyes, and I'm not sure how to handle it. A thing of beauty, a rare and delicate flower with petals so intricate and balanced and seemingly woven together. The Lord somehow saw fit to let me be refreshed with a gift I'm sure not worthy of, something I could have only asked as a dream or a pie-in-the-sky idea. But it happened. And in such a wonderful way.

"I had coffee with a woman tonight. A beautiful creation inside and out. So much that it would embarrass me to describe it because I'd fail to do it justice, and my description would be lacking. Still, my eyes locked with the brown, deep, and dreamy eyes of a woman of purpose and drive tonight, and she was not afraid to keep talking to me. A thirty-eight-year-old brunette, of all things. Such an unbelievable and wonderful time of sitting on her couch today and talking. I didn't expect this, though I have been secretly yearning and longing for such a thing. She was so unbelievably easy to talk to. I must admit that more than once her eyes were so pretty and dreamy that I'm not sure what she said. But I know she is unique. And I've never met anyone who ever talked to me about such things. She asked me if I've ever taken a personality test. Well, knock me silly. We talked about everything under the sun today. And again tonight. So wonderful. So nice. She talked to me about writing down what you want in life. Writing down in detail what you want. So that you pursue it. I left her house and texted my sister, Mary.

"'I'm going to marry her someday.'

"And that's all I'm going to write tonight."

What did I expect or think? Life was rolling in a positive direction, one that I didn't quite know how to treat or handle. It was fresh, exciting, and new. I was enjoying what has happening day by day. What was God doing? I really didn't quite know. All I knew was that it was wonderful, and I wanted more.

Journal entry: January 11, 2019

"How can I explain what has happened, seemingly overnight? I can't. The beauty and blossom is occurring faster than I have time to write it down.

"I met a woman. A very special woman. A bright smile. A beam of fresh sunlight at first dawn. A sparkle in her eyes. The kindest heart. A rose in the center of the sidewalk that I didn't intend to walk past.

"To say that we hit it off well would be an understatement. She mysteriously can connect with my every move. This is a mystery for sure. How long and deep did God have to look to find a thirty-eight-year-old brown-eyed brunette with an insatiable appetite for living life with a smile? One that seemingly fits in the places that I can't complete myself? An author. A motivational masterpiece. A woman I cannot seem to talk to without cracking a smile inside and out. The first spring breeze has been allowed to flow into the window of a stale house window. She is amazing. She is a Christ follower in deed, not just in word. A gypsy. An incredible, attractive, gypsy. She understands why I'm a pirate already. Because she's a gypsy.

"I cannot write fast enough in this book to contain this new discovery.

"A gift. A gift seemingly from the Lord.

"A friend."

"Come to me, all who labor and are heavy laden, and I will give you rest. Take my yoke upon you, and learn from me, for I am gentle and lowly in heart, and you will find rest for your souls. For my yoke is easy, and my burden is light" (Matthew 11:28–30)."

Was this the rest God was providing me? Should I be leery? Should I just enjoy what God was doing? I'll obey the next step, the next day. I'll listen to his voice. I'll live for him.

And hope for his blessings.

Chapter 12
Restoration

No one really knows why they are alive until they know what they'd die for.
~ Martin Luther King Jr.

Like a bubbling smile that cannot wait to express its joy, the beams of light break forth and fill the land with beauty. The dead of night is over; the sun shines once more. In a glorious display of cosmic wonder, it shines in all its splendor, a blazing ball of fire, expressing its bouquet of radiance for all who wait to see. The warm rays of light heat and clothe the land in a new garment, and the earth itself trades the robes of its musty winter blanket for the glory of a new dawn and beginning. In the light of brightness, yellow glows, and orange blazes majesty; life is handed to its awaiting surface, and the valley breaks forth in song once more. Green sprouts of energy emerge everywhere, poking their faces from death to life as the land becomes a meadow in a spectacle of grace.

Grace.

Nothing lost, nothing forgotten, the under-turned nutrients of the past fuel the newfound growth of future hope and grandeur. Strength and dignity paint the fields green with vibrancies. Flowers burst forth in a palette of colored diversity. Blue hues, orange poppies, a lavender effect of splashing balance—they all join, hand in hand to decorate the view I now see. I close my eyes and breathe the scene in deeply. Aromas so delicate and sweet, hinting at what once was, yet in bolder flavor and taste to my senses. I inhale with pleasure. I know from what I smell that life is in full swing. I breathe life in with all the enjoyment and expectation of a good book waiting to be read. Open once more, my eyes are dazzled with a full color spectrum, full of beauty and wonder. I cannot wait to run my feet through it. The forgotten song of brokenness is named as long-past memories of thought. A new era of hope has blossomed forth. My eyes and arms are wide to take it all in. Joy is set before me.

§

During this time, I became increasingly aware that my life had a specific purpose. To live for myself would mean a life less than lived, perhaps wasted, and I would be much happier pleasing the Creator that knit me together than anything I could do for my own self or pride. I wanted not only to achieve it, but to nail it, to rock it. I set out on a course to obey him each and every day that I was blessed to awake. I asked God what *he* wanted, not just what I wanted to do. I not only asked but pleaded with him to reveal his specific purpose to me. I desperately desired to know why he created me and what he intended to do with my life. I began to see that finding God's will for your life wasn't necessarily like a big, bold banner written across the sky with a loud archangel blaring a trumpet and announcing it. Instead, it was a series of small steps as God led you in a direction toward himself. Some of the steps I took might have been so small that I didn't even notice I had taken them, but I was continually moving forward. The progression that my life took toward finding God's will for me was exciting, and I enjoyed following his leading.

I was on a new path, and life was falling into place.

Looking back, I realized that the struggles I faced were exactly what taught me how to be led by God. God leads as a shepherd. When a shepherd leads a little lamb, he walks behind it, using his crook to help guide it. When a lamb goes a little bit off the path, a bump on the side sets the little fellow straight again and keeps him on course. To be led is much different than being carried. When you are led, you are expected to walk, to step, to take action, and to move forward under your own will and desire.

Our Good Shepherd leads us from behind, which was exactly what I let him do. I took steps in faith. I began to walk in the direction that I felt God desired me to go. I couldn't expect God to do everything for me. I had to take the steps of faith and move forward. I walked. I let him bump me onto the correct course when I veered a little too far to the right or the left. He was very kind, gentle, and patient with me. I gave him permission to orchestrate situations. I was excited and wanted to see where he was taking me, and I was happy to be moving in a positive direction.

> So Joseph said to his brothers, "Come near to me, please." And they came near. And he said, "I am your brother, Joseph, whom you sold into Egypt. And now do not be distressed or angry with yourselves because you sold me here, for God sent me before you to preserve life. For the famine has been in the land these two years, and there are yet five years in which there will be neither plowing nor harvest. And God sent me before you to preserve for you a remnant on earth, and to keep alive for you many survivors. So it was not you who sent me here, but God. He has made me a father to Pharaoh, and lord of all his house and ruler over all the land of Egypt. (Genesis 45:4–8)

Did it ever occur to you how amazing it was that in the end, Joseph did not blame or harbor resentment toward his brothers? The truth of the matter was that the Lord had used the hardships of his life to change his perspective and his mindset. He had matured through all the struggles instead of being defeated by them. He was a wiser man now, a refined man of character, possibly even thankful for the difficulties in his life as they were used to make him who and what he was. He could not have achieved his purpose any other way.

> Blessed be the God and Father of our Lord Jesus Christ, the Father of mercies and God of all comfort, who comforts us in all our affliction, so

that we may be able to comfort those who are in any affliction, with the comfort with which we ourselves are comforted by God. For as we share abundantly in Christ's sufferings, so through Christ we share abundantly in comfort too. If we are afflicted, it is for your comfort and salvation; and if we are comforted, it is for your comfort, which you experience when you patiently endure the same sufferings that we suffer. Our hope for you is unshaken, for we know that as you share in our sufferings, you will also share in our comfort.

For we do not want you to be unaware, brothers, of the affliction we experienced in Asia. For we were so utterly burdened beyond our strength that we despaired of life itself. Indeed, we felt that we had received the sentence of death. But that was to make us rely not on ourselves but on God who raises the dead. He delivered us from such a deadly peril, and he will deliver us. On him we have set our hope that he will deliver us again. (2 Corinthians 1:3–10)

I now knew that God would use everything in my life to do the same for me as he had done with Joseph. God was using me, and the struggles of my life had matured me in both faith and trust in my King. No doubt, I was a different man, and I was heading in the direction God wanted me to go. I was allowing him to lead, and my feet weren't afraid to walk. The big question at hand was what God was doing with me now.

Every step was new and uncharted in the journey; I was on a breathtaking adventure that God himself was unveiling before my eyes. The friend God had given me in Faerie became such a vital part of my structure and balance in life. She seemed to meet the parts of me that I lacked or was weak in. God had been speaking to me about her over and over. We were uniquely created for each other. She was a physical representation of the message God had been impressing on me. She pushed me in the ways that God pushed me. She encouraged me in what God already told me to do. Sometimes, she was a voice of reason when I knew what God was speaking to me, but out of fear or worry, I didn't listen to him. She complemented me perfectly.

> Oh give thanks to the Lord, for he is good,
> for his steadfast love endures forever!
> Let the redeemed of the Lord say so,
> whom he has redeemed from trouble
> and gathered in from the lands,
> from the east and from the west,
> from the north and from the south.
>
> Some wandered in desert wastes,
> finding no way to a city to dwell in;
> hungry and thirsty,
> their soul fainted within them.
> Then they cried to the Lord in their trouble,
> and he delivered them from their distress.
> He led them by a straight way
> till they reached a city to dwell in.
> Let them thank the Lord for his steadfast love,
> for his wondrous works to the children of man!
> For he satisfies the longing soul,
> and the hungry soul he fills with good things.

Some sat in darkness and in the shadow of death,
prisoners in affliction and in irons,
for they had rebelled against the words of God,
and spurned the counsel of the Most High.
So he bowed their hearts down with hard labor;
they fell down, with none to help.
Then they cried to the Lord in their trouble,
and he delivered them from their distress.
He brought them out of darkness and the shadow
of death,
and burst their bonds apart.
Let them thank the Lord for his steadfast love,
for his wondrous works to the children of man!
For he shatters the doors of bronze
and cuts in two the bars of iron.

Some were fools through their sinful ways,
and because of their iniquities suffered affliction;
they loathed any kind of food,
and they drew near to the gates of death.
Then they cried to the Lord in their trouble,
and he delivered them from their distress.
He sent out his word and healed them,
and delivered them from their destruction.
Let them thank the Lord for his steadfast love,
for his wondrous works to the children of man!
And let them offer sacrifices of thanksgiving,
and tell of his deeds in songs of joy!

Some went down to the sea in ships,
doing business on the great waters;
they saw the deeds of the Lord,
his wondrous works in the deep.
For he commanded and raised the stormy wind,

which lifted up the waves of the sea.
They mounted up to heaven; they went down to
the depths;
their courage melted away in their evil plight;
they reeled and staggered like drunken men
and were at their wits' end.
Then they cried to the Lord in their trouble,
and he delivered them from their distress.
He made the storm be still,
and the waves of the sea were hushed.
Then they were glad that the waters were quiet,
and he brought them to their desired haven.
Let them thank the Lord for his steadfast love,
for his wondrous works to the children of man!
Let them extol him in the congregation of the
people,
and praise him in the assembly of the elders.

He turns rivers into a desert,
springs of water into thirsty ground,
a fruitful land into a salty waste,
because of the evil of its inhabitants.
He turns a desert into pools of water,
a parched land into springs of water.
And there he lets the hungry dwell,
and they establish a city to live in;
they sow fields and plant vineyards
and get a fruitful yield.
By his blessing they multiply greatly,
and he does not let their livestock diminish.
When they are diminished and brought low
through oppression, evil, and sorrow,
he pours contempt on princes
and makes them wander in trackless wastes;

but he raises up the needy out of affliction
and makes their families like flocks.
The upright see it and are glad,
and all wickedness shuts its mouth.
Whoever is wise, let him attend to these things;
let them consider the steadfast love of the Lord.
(Psalm 107:1–43)

Journal entry: June 17, 2019

"So the Lord heard that prayer. This morning in my regular reading, I came on Psalm 107. How many times, over and over, did the Lord reassure me this way? He hears us in our despair and acts on it. He wants to make sure I understand this recurring theme. 'Oh that man would praise the Lord for His goodness, and for His wonderful works to the children of men!'

I need to praise him. He already has given me the victory in all things by the cross, and when he hears and acts on our behalf, *we need to praise*!

So I'm going to right now."

Psalm 107 is tremendously special to me. I look at who this psalm is written for: those who have wandered in desert wastelands, those who have sat in darkness and in the shadow of death, those who were fools through their sinful ways, and those who went down to the sea in ships, doing business on the great waters. Perhaps if for nobody else, God wrote Psalm 107 for me.

Those are the exact places that I have been in my life, yet in his grace and mercy, he considered me worthy of rescue. Not only did God take me from these places and usher me into safety, but he blessed me in the process. Look at what God does for his anointed in this psalm: "He turns rivers into a desert, springs of water into thirsty ground, a fruitful land into a salty waste, he turns a desert into pools of water, a parched land into springs of water. And there he lets the hungry dwell, and they establish a city to live in; they sow fields and plant vineyards and get a fruitful yield. By his blessing they multiply greatly, and he does not let their livestock diminish."

Wow! Sign me up, coach. I'll take one of those.

On August 11, 2019, on a beautiful, perfect late-summer Sunday, we were wed. The hills were kissed with the golden-hour love of light; the water was delicately graced with soft hues of peace. We had decided to share our marriage union with God alone and the pastor and his wife necessary to seal the service as witnesses. We had each been through marriage twice before, and as adults in mid-life, we chose to not let details and arrangements clutter the beauty of what we felt needed to be cherished only in our hearts and minds. We invited God to be there, to join us in marriage as one. The ceremony seemed more of a prayer service than anything else.

We held hands, asking the one who created us to create something special in our marriage, and pledged our lives to him in reverence. We didn't just want to be married; we wanted God to start something new and relevant. We asked him to join us as one with purpose,

243

and we trusted that would happen. Right there by the water's edge, our lives would start anew. Our lives were not over but were possibly just beginning, which excited us and filled us with satisfaction at the divine redemption that was unfolding. We didn't need to be dressed in a fancy tuxedo or wedding dress. We didn't need a band playing soft songs of love or passion. We had Jesus. We had hope. We had purpose. Neither of us had ever dreamed this was possible: sharing this beauty while the summer sun was setting. After all, our lives were devastated ruins, right? Out of the ashes of two broken lives, God seemed to raise something special, something beautiful, and something priceless.

Journal entry: August 13, 2019

"So what can one liken a moment like this to? What analogy could be made? It is like looking at the cover of an amazing fairytale novel, and once buying it and taking it home, the story is more beautiful than the cover could ever foretell. Or it is possibly like making the trip to the ocean's edge long before the dawn of day in preparation to watch the sunrise, only to be dazzled and amazed when God used the full palette at his disposal and stunned the viewer with awestruck glory.

"That, in essence, is what the last few days have been like. In all honesty, I couldn't have dreamed that being married to Faerie would be this crazy amazing. In every way—emotionally, physically, mentally, and spiritually—God has truly blessed me above anything I could have ever asked or imagined. He has demonstrated our special verse to be rock solid and true. 'Now to Him who is able to do immeasurably more than all we ask or imagine, according to His power that is at work within us, to him be glory in the church and in Christ Jesus throughout all generations, for ever and ever! Amen' (Ephesians 3:20–21).

"He has restored 'all that the locusts have eaten.'

"Praise be to his unspeakable name, power, and praise.

"Thank you, Lord. You have blessed this trip above measure."

Chapter 13
The End of It All

In the end, it's not the years in your life that count. It's the life in your years.
~ Abraham Lincoln

Have you ever come to a place in your life where you look back and wondered how on earth you got there? Have you ever had that moment when you drift off in thought while driving, and after reaching your destination, you wonder how in the world time passed like it did? Sometimes I take a snapshot of my life and take a look at the picture of what it looks like now, thinking these same thoughts. How could I have possibly gotten to where I am today? I look around me. I'm astonished at how God brought me through so much. I sometimes can't believe how he did it, why he loves so much, or why he has turned my life around and blessed me in such rich ways. I'm not a man of money by any means, but the richness that the Lord has opened up to me in intangible ways has made me one of the wealthiest men on earth. I've been through fire and through water, through the stormy seas, and the heat of an iron furnace. This has resulted in a different perspective, an incredibly strong relationship with my heavenly Father, and a now-bulletproof faith. It is a healthy life, one I'm not worthy of.

I drift off and daydream about where I am in life right now. I think of the wonderful blessing I have with Faerie as my wife. It is a love story written by God. How could I have possibly orchestrated something so sweet and perfect in my own strength or imagination? How could I have found someone so suited to my creative nature, someone who pushes me with a positive shove toward a higher calling and more effective ministry? I could have searched for a hundred years and not found a woman that meets me in the unique realm of creativity that my mind often goes to. Not only does she put up with it, but she embraces it. Even more so, she has basically lived a parallel life to mine through the last fifteen years of struggle. Her story is similar to mine. She can identify with much of my pain and the scarring of my heart and mind.

Actually, Faerie went through a lot of it with me. She watched my first wife become sick, and oddly enough, she brought us meals when we needed them. She was there when Becca passed and when the church mourned the loss. She was also overwhelmed by the church split as she had served in a similar capacity as I did. She was a Sunday School teacher, and also served in the women's ministry and the evangelistic outreach team, the Christians In Action (CIA). Like me, she had directed plays. She has written books for children, some of which she intends to publish. She is an artist with a creative flare. She stands fully behind me in my writing and painting passions and understands my need to express myself.

A soldier like me, we were both searching and wandering for quite some time, and interestingly enough, we hit rock bottom at nearly the exact same moment. We were unknowingly and graciously steered back onto the right path by the Lord during the same months as well. Our stories not only inspire others; they inspire us. It is a miracle how God brought us together when he did at just the right moment, even when we weren't really looking to date, find love, or find a mate. If there is anyone who is matched toe-to-toe with me and with who I am, it's Faerie. She is a blessing like no other. I am truly grateful for her and for how God put her in my life.

I think of how our family has been forming. It has been a really amazing and interesting sight to watch God knit the hearts and minds of a broken family together. Blended families share their own set of interesting dilemmas, and God is working and sorting out these matters for us in his way, which is a blessing in itself. I brought two amazing, wonderful, and very special boys into our marriage. She brought one. The incredible privilege of being a stepdad to yet another boy is such a beautiful wonder. I am thankful each and every day that God has allowed me to be an influence in his life to bring him closer to Jesus. I was thrilled to have him around the house when I was bound to a chair for so long. He is a ball of energy and a barrel of fun.

The Lord is by no means finished yet as others are still being interwoven into our family fabric. Many past relationships have been restored. Former hurts and pains have been healed. I never take for granted the healing of people as they thrive and become healthy and balanced. I am truly thankful for this. God has done such an amazing work in our lives, and I hope that continues. I hope that the beautiful patchwork quilt of a family tree can become great and healthy as I'm still waiting for some prayers to be answered and restoration with others I love and care for deeply. I still hope that the relationships with stepchildren from my last marriage can be healthy and strong as God stitched them intentionally together in the same quilt. Some beautiful things I'm still waiting for.

Ministry also is beginning to take flight. We have enjoyed being part of a new church family, and God has begun to use us in the body of Christ. The interaction with other believers is such a salve of healing. We have made many new friends as the Lord has opened doors for us. Someone recently told me that the sweetest moment of impact that they saw in Faerie and me while watching us minister was when we simply held hands, worshipping the Lord. That sight, when you know our past and backgrounds, is a sight of God's power and redemption. Despite everything we've been through as we stand there together, singing our hearts to God inspires others.

While I was bound to a couch, I started a blog at Chuck-Carr.com. One day, I stopped and told my wife, "I never would have thought I would be doing such a thing, not even a year ago." God has transformed me from a man who felt as if he were yesterday's news to be thrown in the trash can to someone who is effectively influencing others for God's glory. I simply cannot believe how far he has brought me. In my wildest dreams, I never thought I'd be a blogger. I never thought that I would be writing my second book in less than a year. If I would have dreamed for a hundred years, I never could have imagined I'd be in this spot today. Now, people from all over the world read and are ministered to through my website.

Do I know where God is taking me? No, I don't have a clue. I'd be silly to even try to put a limit on it. I'd be even more out of my league to try to take a guess, because if God can do something this great when you allow him to, who knows where I'll be when I look back the next time? Can we possibly know God's goodness, what he intends to do with us, and what his future plans are? Some might make an assumption.

To be honest, I can't fathom what God will do next. I'd like to keep writing books and ministering to people. I'd love to inspire others to use their gifts and talents despite hardships. I feel a specific calling on my life to meet hurting people right where they are and to help lift them up and point them to the Lord. Yes, I know my heart, but now I also seem to know the Lord's heart too.

To be brutally honest with you, whether the Lord wants me to write, speak, paint, or minister to others, it's all just sprinkles on the top of my ice cream parfait. The real flavor within is when you are in tune with Jesus, walking with him, and in that sweet spot of fellowship. My wife and I have a verse that exemplifies our relationship and attitude about life. It's simple yet profound, and we keep it tucked in our pocket as a banner or motto for us.

As I mentioned in the previous chapter, our life verse says it so perfectly and effectively. "Now to him who is able to do far more abundantly than all that we ask or think, according to the power at work within us, to him be glory in the church and in Christ Jesus throughout all generations, forever and ever. Amen" (Ephesians 3:20–21). Why would I even attempt to guess at what God will do with me next? It *wouldn't* or *couldn't* ever be sufficient. I can't justify putting a cap on his limitless, perfect creativity. To attempt to outthink the Lord—well, that would be plain silly. No, we can't even imagine the work that God will do in and through us.

Whatever God does, it will be good. It will be *far* better than anything I could even come up with to ask for and *far* better than anything I could dream up on my own. We hold this verse as an anchor in our marriage and relationship, understanding that the Lord truly knows what he's doing, and he's doing a fabulous job. He truly can take anything the dirty old world throws your way and turn it around to be sweet to the taste and beautiful to the eyes. I will testify by my own life that Romans 8:28 is true. If there is any verse of the Bible that we have lived, it is this one. God's Word never fails. "And we know that for those who love God all things work together for good, for those who are called according to his purpose" (Romans 8:28).

Are you called as a Christian? Are you following the Lord and allowing his purpose room to work in your life, desiring a satisfaction that only he can bring? If so, I challenge you to put that verse to the test. Emphatically, without hesitation, I promise you that the words God inspired Paul the apostle to write down for the Romans will hold just as true in your life as they were for them. Can God turn your life around? A better question is: "Will you *allow* him to?"

What will God do with us next? Will our writing and speaking be used to reach the masses? Only God knows for sure. Regardless of what the future brings, all that I want to aim for is to be used for Christ's glory, to be used by God in whatever good he chooses. That alone is fulfillment of life itself. If you are in that place, it doesn't get any better. Enjoy the ride. Taste the sweetness.

When God does something good, he does it *very* good. As an artist, I like to stand back and view my work as I am painting a project. I believe that is why God wanted to pause after each day of creation. I can just picture him in my mind, standing back to admire his work, saying, "That's good . . . very, very good." God is just like that. He covers all the bases and looks deeply into details you and I don't even know exist. When God brought Faerie into our lives, he did something stunning. My new family is a breathtaking thing of beauty, one that does not take away from the beauty of the past.

In God's timing, he astoundingly not only did all that is written in this book and more, but he did it in a way that doesn't rob loved ones from the wonderful memories of the old days. Faerie continually reminds Brad and Justin of the caliber of woman their mother was. She has stepped into their lives to accentuate them, not to rewrite history. God was so faithful to find someone for them who not only respected their past but who strove to mold their future.

The Lord's doings are so intricate as Faerie seems to fit in so well even with my first wife's parents. What a tremendous blessing! She had such amazing favor with them long before I even entered the picture. What crazy details God intertwines! With my own parents, Faerie even came to a missions dinner at their house when they were the head of the Mission's Committee at our old church. The Lord works much better than we could ever dream. With God, nothing is ever lost or forgotten. He is not in the business of fixing problems with cheap or generic Band-Aids. He can work in ways that really heal, rather than just cover or fix temporarily. His ministering words and Spirit are infinitely better at any attempt to heal than you or I could dream up. Yes, God cares about each and *every* detail. I'm sure Bec is smiling in heaven right now at the rebirth of a family in the process of healing. God cares for *everyone's* point of view. She would be happy about the smiles that we are now enjoying. God hasn't forgotten her point of view either.

God is good.

Job saw it, felt it, and witnessed it.

Joseph dreamed it, breathed it, and lived it.

Joel heard it, saw it, and wrote it.

And the Lord restored the fortunes of Job, when he had prayed for his friends. And the Lord gave

Job twice as much as he had before. Then came to him all his brothers and sisters and all who had known him before, and ate bread with him in his house. And they showed him sympathy and comforted him for all the evil that the Lord had brought upon him. And each of them gave him a piece of money and a ring of gold.

And the Lord blessed the latter days of Job more than his beginning. And he had 14,000 sheep, 6,000 camels, 1,000 yoke of oxen, and 1,000 female donkeys. He had also seven sons and three daughters. And he called the name of the first daughter Jemimah, and the name of the second Keziah, and the name of the third Keren-happuch. And in all the land there were no women so beautiful as Job's daughters. And their father gave them an inheritance among their brothers. And after this Job lived 140 years, and saw his sons, and his sons' sons, four generations. And Job died, an old man, and full of days. (Job 42:10–17)

Then the Lord became jealous for his land
and had pity on his people.
The Lord answered and said to his people,
"Behold, I am sending to you
grain, wine, and oil,
and you will be satisfied;
and I will no more make you
a reproach among the nations.
"I will remove the northerner far from you,
and drive him into a parched and desolate land,
his vanguard into the eastern sea,
and his rear guard into the western sea;

the stench and foul smell of him will rise,
for he has done great things.
"Fear not, O land;
be glad and rejoice,
for the Lord has done great things!
Fear not, you beasts of the field,
for the pastures of the wilderness are green;
the tree bears its fruit;
the fig tree and vine give their full yield.
"Be glad, O children of Zion,
and rejoice in the Lord your God,
for he has given the early rain for your
vindication;
he has poured down for you abundant rain,
the early and the latter rain, as before.
"The threshing floors shall be full of grain;
the vats shall overflow with wine and oil.
I will restore to you the years
that the swarming locust has eaten,
the hopper, the destroyer, and the cutter,
my great army, which I sent among you.
"You shall eat in plenty and be satisfied,
and praise the name of the Lord your God,
who has dealt wondrously with you.
And my people shall never again be put to shame.
You shall know that I am in the midst of Israel,
and that I am the Lord your God and there is none
else.
And my people shall never again be put to shame.
(Joel 2:18–27)

Though the world tries to beat us down, either due
to our own mistakes or simply due to man's fallen nature,
God can truly heal and restore all that the locusts have

eaten. There is no shortage of his redemptive power and ability. There is no place too barren for his blessings to once again bring forth a tender sprout, growing into a great meadow of life. If I can reach even one hurting soul with the words of this book, I say to that man, woman, or child that aches for relief today, "Hang on, for the Lord is near. He will restore what the locusts consumed. He will once again rebuild his city." He will pour abundant blessings back into the soul who has been put to the grindstone and learned the lessons explained in this book. We serve a great God, a limitless one, and one who is good above all imagination.

Journal entry: January 14, 2019

"Oh Lord,

"Great is your mercy and your grace. You are better to me than I could ask. You have been with me through every walk of life, from the lowest lows to the highest highs, You stay constant beside me. I read tonight: 'O send out Thy light and Thy truth; let them lead me, let them bring me unto thy holy hill, and to Thy tabernacles' (Psalm 43:3).

"Lord, that this verse may be true to me, to us, to all of us. That you would lead us to yourself as you lead us through life.

"Thank you, dearest Lord.

"Amen."

In Closing

I hope that those who read this book will be inspired by my story. I say this not because I am someone great but quite the opposite. As an ordinary man, I've been taken by God's hand on a very interesting journey of faith. That in itself should bring hope and joy to the hurting people of this world. God took me, an ordinary man, and held my hand. He walked me through each step of this story. He held my hand though I squirmed and complained. He did it as a gentle Father.

All That the Locusts Have Eaten even gives me inspiration when I read it. It gives me courage on hard days. It gives me a proper perspective when life becomes hard. May this story also give you hope, the hope to press in to the Lord and his Scripture when life isn't going the way you planned. May it encourage you to grip God's hand even more tightly when the waves of the sea seem to be especially wild and rough. After all, he created the sea, and he controls it. Thank you for allowing me to share my story with you. I pray you will look to him.

With God there is always hope.

Romans 8:28,
Chuck

Other titles by Chuck Carr:

The Convergence
Where Tragedy + Hope Collide

The Convergence plunges deep into the healing of the human heart and spirit. Lost in tragedy, Weston Tanner sets out on a crash course to find real answers to haunting questions that plague his mind and rob him of inner peace. He loved a woman perfectly, to no avail. After the death of his young, beautiful wife Brooklyn, he cannot come to terms with why God *could* have healed her but did not. He blames God for his loss.

In alternating chapters, the parallel story of Mark Turner is one of epic love, elevating readers to a high position of thought and inspiration. Can these two men's radically different lives converge where healing is possible? This book addresses the hard subjects of suffering, loss, and grief, with thought-provoking insights on hard questions, such as "Why do bad things happen to good people?"

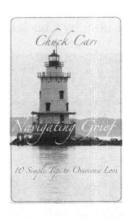

Navigating Grief
10 Simple Tips to Overcome Loss

Grief. Though we all face it, successfully navigating through it is a compelling challenge most fail at. The difficulties of facing loss and coping with its struggle meet us in a place few know what to do with. People of all types can become scarred and frustrated, possibly even blaming God for the losses they are holding. With the help of this booklet, the saddened soul trying desperately to manage grief can one day look back on a healed and healthy individual, living a purpose-filled and abundant life.

Healing is possible. Insights included in this booklet deliver a great head start. As a great gift for those bereaving losses of all kinds, *Navigating Grief: 10 Simple Tips to Overcoming Loss* contains an easy plan for healing of the human heart and spirit.

God has designed his creation to live the abundant life. You can have that. It is in your grasp.

Learn more about Life Compass Ministries at Chuck-Carr.com.
Facebook.com/AuthorChuckCarr.com

Letters to the author can be sent to:
Chuck Carr
P.O. Box 241
Crabtree, PA 15624

Or

Paintwaves7@gmail.com

---

[1] Charles Stanley, *Sharing the Gift of Encouragement* (Nashville: Thomas Nelson, 2008).

[2] C. S. Lewis, *A Grief Observed* (New York: HarperOne, 2001).

[3] "What We Have Once Enjoyed We Can Never Lose ... All That We Love Deeply Becomes a Part of Us," Quote Investigator, accessed August 20, 2020, https://quoteinvestigator.com/2020/05/23/never-lose/.

[4] Anne Lamott, *Anne Lamott Quotes* (Unknown: CreateSpace, 2016).

[5] Max Lucado, *Max On Life: Answers and Insights to Your Most Important Questions* (Plano, TX: Thomas Nelson, 2011).

[6] William Maxwell Hetherington, ed., *Lectures on the Revival of Religion by Ministers of the Church of Scotland* (Glasgow: William Collins, 1840) 374.

[7] Dottie Escobedo-Frank, *Converge Bible Studies: Our Common Sins* (Nashville: Abingdon Press, 2013).

[8] Thomas Manton, D.D., *The Complete Works of Thomas Manton, D.D. with a Memoir of the Author: Volume 14* (London: James Nisbet & Co., 1873), 140.

[9] H. Jackson Brown Jr., "Twenty Years From Now You Will Be More Disappointed by the Things You Didn't Do Than by the Ones You Did Do," accessed August 20, 2020,

https://quoteinvestigator.com/2011/09/29/you-did/.

[10] "He Helped Us With Our Feelings." Mr. Rogers Neighborhood.com, accessed August 20, 2020, https://www.misterrogers.org/articles/he-helped-us-with-our-feelings/.

[11] C. S. Lewis, *The Problem of Pain* (New York: HarperOne, 2001), 141.

[12] George Eliot, *Daniel Deronda* (Edinburgh: William Blackwood and Sons, 1878).

[13] Dieter F. Uchtdorf, "A Matter of a Few Degrees," The Church of Jesus Christ of Latter-Day Saints.com, accessed August 21, 2020, https://www.churchofjesuschrist.org/study/general-conference/2008/04/a-matter-of-a-few-degrees?lang=eng.

[14] Charles H. Spurgeon, *The Complete Works of C. H. Spurgeon, Volume 6 Sermons 286-347* (Harrington, DE: Delmarva Publications, 2015).

[15] "About The Enneagram Institute®," The Enneagram Institute.com, accessed August 21, 2020, https://www.enneagraminstitute.com/about.

Made in United States
Orlando, FL
13 July 2022

19728810R00147